HIDING IN P

Tom Bijvoet

Hiding in Plain Sight

Reflections on the Dutch Presence
in Canada and the USA
1609 to today

Mokeham Publishing Inc. – 2022
P.O. Box 35026, Oakville, ON L6L 0C8, Canada
P.O. Box 559, Niagara Falls, NY 14304, USA
www.mokeham.com

ISBN: 978-1-7774396-9-9

Contents

Introduction

In 1609, as he was searching for the Northwest Passage to Asia on behalf of the *Dutch East India Company*, Henry Hudson sailed up the river that now bears his name. That was the start of the Dutch settlement of North America. Between 1609 and 1621, the year the *Dutch West India Company* decided to establish a permanent colony in the fertile lands that Hudson had explored, Dutch pioneers laid the groundwork for what would become New Netherland. As the colony got established, others joined the fledgling settlement from the Netherlands, and the middle years of the 17th century saw the first wave of Dutch immigration to North America.

The second major wave of Dutch immigration came in the middle of the 19th century. After a split in the Dutch Reformed State Church in 1834, the seceders found that their prospects in the Netherlands, which was suffering from economic stagnation as it was, were poor. Several groups of them decided to move to America for its freedom of religion and its economic opportunities. In 1847 one group established a Dutch seceders' colony in Michigan and founded the town of Holland. The same year another group of seceders founded the town of Pella in Iowa. It was symbolically named for the city in Jordan, where 1st century Christians from Jerusalem found refuge. From Holland and Pella these pioneers fanned out and established additional colonies in Illinois, Wisconsin, Iowa, the Dakotas and Washington.

Almost one hundred years later, the third and thus far final major wave of Dutch immigration washed over North America's shores. The Netherlands lay in ruins after the devastation of five years of German occupation during World War II. Economic prospects were limited, housing was in extremely short supply and there was a sense of dread about the menace of a Soviet inva-

7

sion. The Dutch and Canadian governments initiated a program to entice as many people as possible to move across the ocean and settle in Canada, which needed farm laborers. Hundreds of thousands left the country. Most of them settled in Canada, but the USA also saw a steady flow of Dutch immigrants in the decade after World War II.

Interspersed between these three major movements of Dutch settlers across the ocean there was always a steady trickle of individuals seeking opportunities in the vast space of the North American continent. And at times, depending on circumstances both in the old country and the new, a trickle would become a sizeable stream. Desperate economic conditions in northern Friesland saw whole towns empty out between the 1880s and the start of World War I as their inhabitants found their way across the ocean. In the 1920s Dutch farmers flocked to the fertile lands around Artesia in Southern California and established a bustling dairy industry. After Indonesia gained its independence and when Dutch-Indonesians and Eurasians were expelled in 1959, many of them came to California. Under pressure from milk quotas and other restrictions Dutch dairy farmers came to the Canadian provinces of Ontario and Alberta in large numbers in the 1990s.

These Dutch immigrants, who came to Canada and the USA seeking a better life for themselves and their children left their mark. Because of the long periods that elapsed between the three major immigration waves, and because of the limited numbers that came in between, there is no continuity in the Dutch presence in North America. Whenever a group of new immigrants encountered the descendants of an earlier wave, they found that the differences between the two groups far exceeded any commonalities. In a way, each group had to start over again, without much help from earlier settlers.

The number of Dutch immigrants has always been relatively low compared to those from other European nations, such as

Ireland and Italy. This meant that the Dutch were much less visible. They also often had agricultural backgrounds, so in general they settled in sparsely populated rural areas, rather than forming compact urban communities. Nevertheless, for those who have an eye for these things, the signs of a Dutch presence in North America are abundant. You just need to know where to look.

This is something that became apparent to me when I came to British Columbia from the Netherlands in 1999. As most Dutch people in the home country, I had a vague awareness of the history of the Dutch in North America. But emigration is not a subject that is taught in Dutch history classes. It was with great surprise that I discovered the prevalence of institutions established by the wave of the 1950s in British Columbia, including stores, social clubs, churches, schools, radio programs and newspapers. When we arrived, there were three Dutch language newspapers still being published in Canada. I got in touch with the editor of one of them, *De Hollandse Krant*, and offered to write a monthly column giving a newcomer's perspective. After writing for the paper for almost a decade, I acquired it in 2008 when its publishing editor announced his retirement. I am still publishing it today.

Because the Dutch immigrants of the 1950s had integrated so successfully, and because the number of fluent Dutch readers was declining, I felt that there was a potential for a periodical about the Netherlands and the Dutch, but written in English. So in 2011 I launched *DUTCH the magazine* with the tagline 'About the Netherlands and its people, at home and abroad'. This book focuses on the 'abroad' part of the tagline.

In 2013 we moved the business – and the family – from British Columbia to Ontario, where the largest number of Dutch immigrants to Canada and their descendants live.

In this book I have collected the articles that I have contributed to the magazine, which cover aspects of the Dutch presence in the USA and Canada. The subjects I tackled are varied and cover all major immigration waves.

This book does not present a linear, or comprehensive history of the Dutch presence in North America. The essays, columns and feature articles brought together in this book, all of which have previously been published in the magazine, focus on specific elements of the Dutch presence in North America. Together, I hope that they give a sense of what it means and meant to be Dutch in North America. For more in-depth explorations of specific topics, I refer to the bibliography. Many excellent books have been written about aspects of the Dutch presence in the USA and Canada. I hope that this book can serve as a guideline for topics to be explored in more detail.

I have grouped the articles in three sections, which I have called *Identification*, *Exploration* and *Reflection*. The Identification section contains personal columns, about adapting to life in my new country and discovering what it means to be a Dutch-Canadian. In Exploration I investigate topics related to the history and culture of the Dutch presence in North America over the centuries. And finally in Reflection I have collected mini-biographies of notable Dutch North-American or North-American Dutch individuals. In every issue of *DUTCH the magazine* we highlight the life of someone who has impacted society in one way or another and who has recently died. I have collected the obituaries of the people we profiled, who came to North America from the Netherlands, or moved in the opposite direction. Taken together they give an interesting flavor of what it means at an individual level to be an immigrant and straddle two cultures, and what motivates people to cross the ocean in search of a new life.

The articles have only been lightly edited from their original form, where inclusion in a book, rather than a magazine, called for adaptation. I have also removed any glaring duplications in the text across the different articles collected in the book. But otherwise the articles appear as they did in their original form in the magazine. I have ordered the articles logically and thematically, which means that they do not appear in the order in which they were orginally published. The date of first publication is given with each article.

I hope to continue exploring the Dutch presence in North America in years to come and have several interesting road trips planned, about which I will report in the magazine. And in case you had missed that, that's a sales pitch. You can subscribe to *DUTCH the magazine* on our dutchthestore.com website. Enjoy the book!

The Netherlands and Holland
a Disclaimer

The Netherlands is not the same as Holland. I know. The use of the term 'Holland' to refer to 'the Netherlands' always invites discussion, and I may as well get the issue out of the way right here.

Historically only two of the twelve provinces of the current Kingdom of the Netherlands should be referred to as Holland: the provinces of North and South Holland. They occupy by and large the same area as the former county of Holland, the most powerful of the lands that formed the Low Countries of old. Over the years in general parlance the name denoting the old powerful County of Holland has come to be applied to the entire territory of the Kingdom of the Netherlands. This is sometimes resented by people from the other provinces. In consideration of these sensitivities we changed the name of our Dutch language monthly newspaper from *De Hollandse Krant* (The Hollandish Newspaper) to *Maandblad de Krant* (The Newspaper Monthly) – *De Krant* for short – when we purchased the title in 2008. It is editorial policy of De Krant to use the term 'Nederland' exclusively and consistently, except when the text clearly and explicitly refers to Holland and Holland alone. But De Krant is written in Dutch and this book is written in English and it is there that an important distinction lies. I believe that in English 'Holland' is a legitimate term for the country that is known officially as 'The Kingdom of the Netherlands'. If one says in English to someone from any country other than the Netherlands that one hails from Holland, the conclusion is not that one comes from one of the two western provinces. Even people who know the Netherlands well, will not blink an eyelid if the response to the follow-up question 'what part of Holland?' is 'Groningen', 'Brabant' or 'Limburg'. This usage stems, in my opinion, not from the arrogance of the true Hollanders, but likely from the grammatical awkwardness of the 'correct' term. Should 'the Netherlands' take a singular or a plural verb form, for instance? Well, plural one would say, but on the other hand, is 'the Netherlands' not simply an abbreviation of 'The Kingdom of the Netherlands', which would take the singular. Besides, very few countries take a definite article, which adds to the awkwardness.

A similar, but reverse process – where not as in the case of Holland a part has given its name to the whole, but where the whole has given its name to a part – has taken place with 'the United States of America', another accurate name which is unwieldy in a text that has to flow easily, and it is often substituted simply with 'America'. Most Canadians (who if we wish to be precise are Americans too) take no issue with referring to citizens of the United States as 'Americans', but many Latin-Americans resent the usage.

In addition, 'the Netherlands' historically is an incorrect term to refer to the territory of the current Kingdom. Taken the true historical interpretation, the Netherlands encompass Belgium and even parts of Northern Germany. So by outlawing 'Holland' and substituting it exclusively with 'the Netherlands' I would be replacing one technically incorrect term with another.

Even the 'Kingdom of the Netherlands' as a descriptor presents issues. From 1813 until 1831 the kingdom included what are now Belgium and Luxembourg, with the status of the current Dutch province of Limburg not settled until 1867. And after World War II, in constellations that varied over the years, the kingdom included Dutch possessions in the West-Indies. Currently the Kingdom of the Netherlands consists of four countries 'Sint Maarten', 'Curaçao' and 'Aruba' in the Caribbean and 'Nederland' which comprises the European portion of the kingdom and three other islands in the Caribbean (Bonaire, Sint Eustatius and Saba), which are considered 'public bodies' (a special type of municipalities) of 'Nederland'. Yes, it all is arcane and confusing.

So the next time I write 'Holland' and mean what most people would associate with the term, please forgive me. To be more accurate I should have written 'The post-1839 European territories of the Kingdom of the Netherlands'. Having taken all of the above into careful consideration, I have decided to use 'the Netherlands' and 'Holland' interchangeably and as synonyms in this book. I intend no disrespect to people from the other provinces, but simply wish to keep it simple by following long-established usage.

September/October 2011

IDENTIFICATION

Hiding in Plain Sight

I was driving along the *Queen Elizabeth Way (QEW)*, the highway that follows the shore of Lake Ontario from Toronto to close to the US border at Fort Erie. This stretch of road forms the backbone of what has become known as the 'Golden Horseshoe', the industrious, wealthy region that includes such great manufacturing and service centers as Toronto, Mississauga, Oakville, Burlington, Hamilton, and St. Catharines. It also happens to be the region where a vast number of Dutch immigrants settled in the 1950s and 1960s, and where *DUTCH the magazine* set up shop in 2013.

Paul, a Canadian friend of mine, was traveling with me, and as we were driving along the busy highway, I found myself following a car with a personalized license plate that read 'Keunink'. "Dutch," I said to him. "What?" he said. "Oh, just the name on that plate, it's a Dutch name."

"I suppose you don't meet a lot of your compatriots here, do you?" he mused, as we drove by the huge *Voortman Cookies* plant in Burlington.

"Well, funny you should say that..." I replied. "As the publisher of a magazine that caters to people interested in the Netherlands and the Dutch, I have made it my business to meet and recognize Dutch people and, in all honesty, that is not very hard to do here. There are more Dutch people hidden in plain sight than you might think."

"Really..." Paul continued. I think he seemed genuinely interested, in a polite, multicultural, inclusive Canadian sort of way. "I never knew that."

"Well," I replied, "we don't stand out, really. We're not what you would call a visible minority. Besides, the Dutch integrate very quickly. Most of the original immigrants can be recognized by their accent, although it is surprising how few people can place it. Strangely enough, we are often mistaken for French-Canadians, or – and this always causes huge embarrassment to Canadians with a sense of history – Germans. But many of the kids, the second generation, only have a passive understanding of Dutch. We tend to intermarry. There are no Dutch neighborhoods in cities like Toronto, and we don't go in for ethnic festivals or events in a big way."

We had left the highway to run a few errands, and as I drove along Harvester Road in Burlington, we passed a small model windmill in the front yard of a building proudly proclaiming to belong to *De Boer Poultry*. "Okay, that makes sense," Paul replied. "But isn't it also because there are relatively few of you? Holland is a small country after all, and you must be vastly outnumbered by other immigrant groups."

Although I was beginning to feel a little bad about having to contradict him again, I pointed out that although people of Dutch descent are outnumbered by groups that have immigrated en masse in recent decades (such as Indians, Chinese and Jamaicans), up until the 1970s the Dutch were the fifth largest ethnic group in Canada, after only the 'home' nations of Britain and France, First Nations and Germans. Despite the high visibility of the Italian, Portuguese and Greek communities in Toronto, more Dutch immigrants came to Canada in the postwar decades than any of those nationalities. I turned back onto the QEW as we passed a shopping mall with a sign that read *Goemans Appliances*. "Actually half a million Ontarians claimed to be of Dutch descent in the most recent census."

"Okay that's a good-sized number…" Paul had to agree.

"Yes, and probably half of those live in the extended Golden Horseshoe area. So a license plate with a Dutch name should only be a surprise in the sense that as a frugal people we don't commonly tend to splurge on luxuries such as vanity plates." Paul grinned.

We zipped by *De Wildt's Honda* dealership on the South Service Road that runs parallel to the highway.

"You know I should be on the lookout a little more," Paul said, as we exited the highway just past a large office building with the name *Berendsen* on it in prominent letters.

"Let's grab a bite for lunch," I said.

Paul agreed: "I know a fine Italian place, or do you prefer Greek or Indian?"

"Nah ... let me take you somewhere."

I parked the car in front of a store that had displays of windmills and tulips in the window, and we walked in. We sat down at a small round table, and I ordered a cup of pea soup and a croquette on a bun for each of us. "Enjoy!" I said, when the waitress brought our lunch. By then Paul had worked out that the 2000-square-foot store specialized in Dutch groceries. "This is big, you're right, there must be a fair number of Dutch people here to sustain such a store."

"Yes, and there is another really big one in Roseland Plaza in Burlington and one in St. Catharines on Ontario Street and in Waterdown and in Hamilton and Beamsville and ..."

"Yes, I get the picture," Paul said, "but what is that delicious breaded sausage thingy called again...?"

May/June 2014

Disappearing Dutchness

According to the latest census figures, about one million Canadians claim Dutch descent. That represents one out of every thirty-five Canadians. That may not sound like a lot, but if you think about it in practical terms, it really is. It means that on a daily basis you will encounter Dutch-Canadians, often without realizing it. That friendly barista at Starbucks, the high school music teacher, the secretary at the office, the electrician, the family doctor (all true examples from my own experience): Dutch.

Although generally invisible, sometimes the telltale signs are there, but only if you know where to look. One New Year's Eve we attended a potluck party at a friend's house in rural remote Penticton, British Columbia. The dining room table was filled with typical Canadian fare: Nanaimo bars, Timbits, the ever-present bread bowl with spinach dip, chips and salsa. Amid all the standard North American stuff I noticed a platter stacked with what looked like 'oliebollen' (deep-fried dough balls). Real Dutch oliebollen. I picked one up and took a careful bite. It was the genuine article. It took some asking around, but eventually I tracked down the person who had brought them. He explained that his father-in-law, who was indeed Dutch, always made them by the dozens on New Year's Eve. He was not even aware of the cultural significance and thought that it was a quirk isolated to his father-in-law. He had only brought them because they could not get rid of them all otherwise.

One day, driving the four hundred kilometers back from Vancouver to Penticton, I pulled off the highway in the tiny town of Hope (the last stop before the mountains) to get gas. After filling up, I took a wrong turn and pulled into the parking lot of a small, run-down strip mall to get my bearings. As I looked through the windscreen, I noticed a sun-faded poster with windmills and tulip fields in one of the shop windows. Curious, I got out of the car and peered in – it was after seven at night, and the stores in the mall were closed. It was a bakery. Behind the counter inside, I noticed a sign announcing 'genuine European baked goods – Dutch apple pie and almond cookies'.

Occasionally, you will see a little model windmill in a front yard, or a wooden shoe nailed to the siding of a house, or, during World Cup soccer season, little orange *KNVB* (*Koninklijke Nederlandse Voetbal Bond* – Royal Dutch Soccer Association) flags mounted on cars. The times when, as is reputed, you would hear more Dutch on a Saturday afternoon in downtown Grimsby, Ontario than English, are long gone. The 200,000 Dutch nationals who arrived in Canada in the 1950s integrated fast and successfully, and their descendants intermarried with Canadians of other ethnic heritage. The Dutchness of Dutch-Canadians has diluted fast. Typical expressions of Dutchness are becoming increasingly rare. In the seventeen years since I came to Canada, I have witnessed a number of harbingers of the loss of Dutch culture. Gradually, Dutch products started disappearing from the ethnic food aisles of mainstream supermarkets. One sad day I noticed that the *BC Liquor Store* in Penticton had stopped selling *Boomsma* Jenever. And now, with sadness we see another one of those hidden gems disappear.

It was one of those many subliminal Dutch landmarks in Canada. A men's clothing store in a strip mall in suburban Burlington, Ontario. *Filman's Men's Wear.* The storefront gave nothing away, but once inside, the careful observer would notice the posters of Dutch liberation commemorations, the books and DVDs about Princess Margriet, 'friendship ties' with Dutch and Canadian, and Dutch and American flags, and the Dutch iconography in citations on the wall for the store's owner, Jack van der Laan, in recognition of the tireless work he did to promote Dutch-Canadian friendship. Jack was also a staunch supporter of *DUTCH the magazine,* and he would always have some at hand in the store and in his car to give to interested clients and relations. Jack, the founder of the *Canada Netherlands Friendship Association,* was a driving force behind the twinning of his adopted hometown of Burlington with the Dutch city of Apeldoorn, and instrumental in getting Burlington to institute a *Canada Netherlands Friendship Day* on May 5th in honor of the Canadian involvement in the liberation of the Netherlands. Jack has announced his retirement, and is closing the store. With that decision, another little hidden piece of Dutch-Canadian heritage is sadly lost.

January/February 2017

What I really miss…

When I first came to Canada, my friends in Holland always wanted to know what Dutch things I missed most in my new country. That there was something I should miss was never in doubt; it was just a question of what. This subject came up so often that I had a rehearsed answer: "*BBC* television on cable, *Orval* beer, mozzarella made by Tozzi, Moksi on a bun, the *Falafel King* and Restaurant *Bojo*." The first reaction was generally one of recognition: "Yes, imaginable, good stuff all of that." Until the inevitable realization came: "But none of that is Dutch!" Of course, I was only doing it to tease them a little, and I would be lying if I said there was nothing Dutch that I missed.

What I really missed (and occasionally still miss) is fish, certain very specific types of fish that are intricately linked with growing up in Holland and which give one a strange sense of pride in one's heritage. I like bitterballen (deep-fried, ragout-filled balls), croquettes and stroopwafels (syrup-filled wafers) as much as the next person, but I can quite easily do without them and won't necessarily rush to the front of the fray when they are served at consular receptions. However, a tray of salted herring … that's a different story.

In the May/June 2012 issue of *DUTCH the magazine* we ran a full feature on herring and its cultural significance to the Netherlands. That significance is so fundamental to the Dutch psyche that almost every visitor to Holland runs the risk of being dragged to a 'haringkraam' (herring stand) by their host at some point during their stay. I must admit that I subjected quite a few foreign guests to the dubious delight of eating a salted herring at a roadside stand – to their dismay, in many cases. Being sensitive to the fact that some people may not like to hold a raw fish by the tail and then slide it down their throat headfirst, I would magnanimously order them served in the other standard variety: cut up on a small rectangular cardboard platter, with a Dutch flag cocktail stick to eat the pieces of herring with.

A shock to new visitors in many cases, but my good friend Robert from Scotland was not so easily tricked. He had been to Holland before and when I announced, without being specific, that I was going to treat him to a very special local delicacy, he said: "There is no way you are making me eat raw fish!" This was of course before sushi became popular worldwide.

However, we went to the herring stand anyway and, instead of herring, I offered him some smoked eel on a bun. Again he declined, uttering some choice words about Dutch cuisine, and made his way to a French fry place across the street. I ordered the eel on a bun for myself. And now we are getting into territory that comes very close to the true answer I should have given my friends from Holland. If there is one single item that I truly miss in Canada, it is smoked eel.

Eel, a bottom feeder, does not have the most appetizing diet itself. That, and its similarity to a snake, may explain why many people would rather give it a miss. And watching the 'horse head scene' from the *Palme d'Or* winning German film *The Tin Drum* (you can find it on *YouTube*, not for the queasy), might certainly put off a lot of people.

It doesn't stop me though. That probably goes back to the time when my mother, who loved a nice bit of smoked eel, would occasionally buy a bunch, lay them out on newspapers on the kitchen table and tell us to tuck in. Just remove the skin and nibble the flesh off the long backbone. Nirvana was the time during my youth when my parents owned a cabin in Makkum, a seaside town in Friesland, where our next-door neighbor, old man Poepjes, smoked his own eel. There was always some for us!

During my university days in Scotland, I had an interesting experience. One day some of my friends and I found ourselves in a frozen food store. At the time, shops dedicated exclusively to frozen foods were quite a novelty, at least in Scotland. As we were looking around, I came upon a freezer that was filled to the brim with only one product: frozen smoked eel, about four pieces to a package, imported from Holland. I literally shouted in surprised delight: "Smoked eel!" I said jubilantly. "Uggh," said my friends. I explained to the store clerk that I had been in Scotland for several years and had never known they ate smoked eel. "We don't," said the clerk. My friends vigorously nodded their heads in agreement.

I looked at the shop assistant, looked at the freezer, looked back at her and raised my eyebrows. "The eel was shipped to us by central warehouse," she said. "We don't know what they were thinking, and we don't know what to do with the stuff." Alas, we did not have a proper freezer in our student dorm, so I bought only two or three packages at a knock-down price, wished my mother was around to get some, and enjoyed a fine meal of smoked eel. None of my friends seemed to want any (jellied eel is only a Cockney thing that most certainly has not caught on north of the border).

And now…? Well, I have finally persuaded our local European Market owner (second generation Portuguese) that there is more to seafood than bacalhau, sardines and squid, and he now orders frozen smoked eel. It's an expensive predilection; one of the reasons he would not stock it before. He simply could not imagine anyone buying it, especially not at the price it commands. But a few days ago, when I had one of my occasional cravings, he told me that the smoked eel was very popular, and he thanked me for talking him into carrying it in his store. So now, when people ask me what I miss most from Holland, I can honestly say: "From Holland nothing significant, we have smoked eel here in British Columbia."

July/August 2013

Christmas Shopping

About six weeks before our first Christmas in British Columbia, we noticed that people came to focus their conversations on one specific topic: "Have you started your Christmas Shopping yet?" This seemed to be the question that everyone asked us and each other. When I first heard the question, from a colleague, my spontaneous reaction was "no, of course not!". It 'flooped' out (as the Dutch so evocatively say) and probably sounded quite rude to my colleague's polite Canadian ears. She reacted not so much defensively, or hurt, but more puzzled. Of course, it was possible, likely even, that someone (a male especially) had not yet started their Christmas shopping, but why would they say 'of course'?

Having witnessed the incredulity on my colleague's face, henceforth I would respond to the question a bit more tactfully. I'd just raise my shoulders and say "not yet, no" with something that approached a sigh, although I had no idea why it was so important to have started shopping. I usually did it on Christmas Eve, or the day before if I was particularly organized.

About three weeks later the question seemed to generally shift from "Have you started…" to "Ready for Christmas yet?" A question that I did not even understand. "Oh yes, we have the tree up," I answered. It was the only activity I could imagine that was necessary to prepare for the occasion, more than two weeks out. But again, my Canadian friends and neighbors seemed not to understand the casual nature of my reaction. They looked frazzled and frenzied and were looking for a sympathetic ear rather than something that they probably took as uncalled-for sarcasm.

Three days before Christmas my boss asked me what I had bought my wife Petra for Christmas. I replied: "Nothing yet, there's plenty of time." Panic showed in his eyes. I think he valued me as an employee and wanted the best for my personal welfare. He did not need a subordinate with marital issues, so he looked at his watch. "It's almost lunchtime," he said. "Take the rest of the day off and buy her something nice. Something really nice!"

So I left the office, wandered downtown, sat down behind the window of a coffee shop and watched the good citizens of my new home town rush up and down the sidewalks with big shopping bags and boxes in their hands as I ordered lunch.

I had discovered a little shop that stocked specialty greeting cards. Not the run of the mill *Hallmark* or Dollar Store variety, with a cheesy picture and a schmaltzy rhyme, but little works of art. Expensive too, upwards of seven, eight dollars, some even more than ten. After I finished my lunch, I went in and found one that was perfect for Petra. I bought it and thought to myself: 'Great! Now I'm ready for Christmas.'

The company I worked for had the tradition (now defunct because of liability, health and safety issues) to have all staff gather in the boardroom for a glass of wine on Christmas Eve at 3 p.m., before letting everyone leave early. We had done our grocery shopping the day before. I sat contentedly next to my colleague Bruce. He asked me what I had bought my wife for Christmas. "A card," I replied. He looked impressed, whistled between his teeth and said: "Sweet. What kind of car?"

"No, a carDDDDD," I replied, emphasizing the 'D'.

He laughed... "Yeah sure, but what else?"

"Nothing," I replied.

Poor Bruce. He almost seemed to deflate, because a car may have impressed him, but a card and only a card impressed him a whole lot more.

I could tell that this was not the time to go into details about the difference between Dutch and North American Christmas. That in Holland, Petra and I had not given each other presents at Christmas time either, that that was what Sinterklaas, birthdays and anniversaries were for, and that for us, Christmas was a much more spiritual event, centered on quiet contemplation and family time.

That first Christmas in Canada was an interesting cultural experience for us. Of course, we knew from television and film that North Americans focus a lot of their time on buying and giving presents. But the sheer time and effort that involves for a lot of people – and the amount of money – were a revelation.

As residents of Canada with four school-age children, it has been impractical not to join in to some extent. You can hardly send your kids back to school after Christmas break without any trophies show off. But we still keep it simple and focus our time on enjoying the spirit of the season, rather than the consumerist spoils of it.

November/December 2013

Some More Shopping

I do not like the early darkness of November and December. Those are two months that draw me into a melancholic mood which I would just as soon do without. For some reason it seemed to affect me more in British Columbia than it did in the Netherlands. It may have been the low dark skies of the Okanagan Valley where we lived, that made the season feel interminably gloomy, even during the day. We had mountains on either side of us, and in winter the so-called 'valley cloud' came down low and rested on the mountain crests as a kind of lid over the valley. I quite literally felt boxed in. Many people who move to the Okanagan from the prairies feel the same. However cold it may get on the other side of the Rockies, they say, at least the sky is blue and the sun shines.

Of course, the Netherlands is no tropical paradise. The weather there tends to be even more miserable in November and December than it is in the interior of British Columbia, where at least generally it is dry.

But I do not remember those months as gloomy during my youth or even my early working life. From the day Sinterklaas arrived in the country in mid-November until the Christmas tree bonfire just after Epiphany, there was always something to enjoy, to look forward to, or to use as an excuse to have a bit of a party.

The televised official welcome of Saint Nicholas arriving by steamer from Spain kicked off the season. It was followed, usually a week later, by his arrival in your hometown, on horseback, accompanied by the local marching band. Then there were the planned and unplanned visits by Saint Nicholas or his helpers; he visited your school, your place of work and your home on several occasions, either to leave a small gift in a shoe set out by the chimney (or more commonly these days, one of the central heating system radiators) or to toss candy into the house. Then on December 5th everyone was allowed to leave school or work early, often with an employer-supplied almond letter. Families got together to exchange gifts wrapped in a home-crafted 'surprise' together with a pointed poem gently mocking some character trait of the recipient, or to wait for a large sack of presents to be delivered by Saint Nicholas or one of his staff.

The following week the Christmas tree came out, and the Sinterklaas songs which played in malls and shopping streets made way for traditional Christmas carols. Christmas was a quiet family affair, with or without church attendance on Christmas Eve and Christmas Day depending on one's religious affiliation. The afternoon generally included a family activity such as a long walk in the woods, or board games, followed by a festive family dinner. And Boxing Day, when stores were still closed, was often a rerun of Christmas Day with the other set of grandparents or in-laws, strict rotas being adhered to within families ensuring from year to year that the attention of children and grandchildren was divided fairly. Fittingly, the Dutch name for Boxing Day is 'Tweede Kerstdag' (Second Christmas Day).

And between Christmas and New Year, when the kids were still out of school and many adults still off work, 'oliebollen' were made and fireworks and champagne were purchased in the run-up to New Year's Eve. The kids were woken up just before midnight and people headed out into the streets, glass of champagne in hand, to set off fireworks and wish their neighbors a happy New Year. Sometime during the first week in the New Year most companies would have a 'Nieuwjaarsborrel' (New Year's drink) for their staff, where the CEO spoke about the year ahead and where champagne and appetizers were served. And then, after Epiphany, in many neighborhoods people lit bonfires using the dismantled Christmas trees which had been collected door to door. By this time, the days were lengthening and although it may still have been cold and damp, at least things were moving in the right direction.

I honestly don't want to be negative about my new homeland, which I love dearly and its traditions which I cherish, but I cannot help thinking that the period I described above plays out more like this in North America: Thanksgiving: big turkey dinner. Black Friday: shop, shop, shop. Christmas: lots of expensive presents, big turkey dinner. Boxing Day: shop some more. New Year's Eve: let's watch others celebrate on TV. New Year's Day: back to business as usual.

November/December 2014

Not Acceptable
to the US government

In 1989, an eighty-page self-published booklet called *The Undutchables: An Observation of the Netherlands, Its Culture and Its Inhabitants* saw the light. It was written by Laurie Boucke and Colin White, American and English respectively, who boasted a combined total of twenty-two years of self-imposed exile among the Dutch. It was a runaway success. *The European*, a short-lived English-language broadsheet, called it 'a cult among English-speaking expatriates'.

At the time, the Netherlands hosted a large expatriate yuppie Anglophone community, which had descended mainly on Amsterdam and The Hague, attracted by the many multinationals and the liberal liquor licensing laws. On the other side of the economic spectrum, the unwillingness of the Dutch to perform strenuous labor in the construction industry had drawn a significant number of Irish tradesmen to the country. So the book fell on fertile ground. The authors light-heartedly described many typically Dutch quirks that had the Anglos nod in delighted recognition and the Dutch smile and admit, sheepishly sometimes, that the authors were uncannily accurate about their culture and behavior.

As the world changed and Holland changed with it, the authors, living in the United States by now, kept updating the book, adding new information. The page count grew and where the first, almost pamphlet-like edition had about eighty pages, the latest version – the ninth edition, published in November 2019 – has more than 300 pages.

In the early days of the Internet, the Undutchables website drew a crowd of regulars to its bulletin board where all things Dutch were up for discussion. For half a decade or more, regulars ranted and raved and joked about life among the 'cloggies'. Many of the most profound comments posted on the bulletin board made it into later editions of the book.

I was reminded of all this recently when I had to cross the border into the USA from Canada. I presented the import papers for the copies of *DUTCH the magazine* and the *Dutch in Wartime* books that I had with me to mail in the United States. The US border guard studied the documentation carefully, looked at me sternly and, pointing at my signature, said: "What is this?" I replied: "My signature, sir."

He was clearly annoyed and said: "That's not a signature, that's a chicken scratch. It's not acceptable." I really did not know what to say, it looked as if he was serious. In fact, he was serious. "That signature is not acceptable to me, I represent the United States government, so that signature is not acceptable to the United States government," he added, presumably to ensure I understood the gravity of the situation.

For the previous five years I had crossed the border weekly with immigration papers bearing my signature. Never before had I been informed that my signature was unacceptable to the US government, so, presuming that the border guard in question would not truly pursue this any further, I remained polite.

On my many trips across I have generally been treated fairly, but there have been occasions where guards, for whatever reason, felt the need to wield the power their uniform bestows upon them. So I swallowed hard, and stopped myself from saying what I would have liked to say: that none of his colleagues had ever taken issue with my signature, and that it had never stopped me from obtaining and signing passports, driver's licenses, credit cards, titles to real estate, binding contracts and so on. Maybe if I had had a copy of The Undutchables with me, I could have quoted from page 139: 'A Dutch paraaf (signing of initials) consists of one or more large illegible scribbles used mainly to ensure that no one except the originator can decipher the initials. The formal signature (handtekening, lit. hand drawing) is equally as enigmatic as the initials, only there is more of it.'

But I did not have the book with me. The border guard told me to be on my way and change my signature before my next visit to the USA.

I keep a copy of The Undutchables in my glove compartment now, just in case. It may even come in handy with traffic cops. Under the section entitled 'Dutch rules of the road' the book says: 'At least two cars should go through each red light, avoid at all cost reducing speed or stopping'. Well, maybe not, but at least rereading the book as I sit waiting in the long line at the border gives me something to smile about.

January/February 2014

Tractor Skill Games
and Other Diversions

Please close this magazine and look carefully at the bottom right-hand side of the cover. It reads '50'. Yes, that's right. Against all odds and against well-intended advice from industry professionals not to launch a magazine about the Netherlands, we are still around and have produced fifty issues of *DUTCH the magazine* since the fall of 2011. One of the biggest challenges is to get people to find out about us. All too often I encounter people who say: "This is great. I wish I had known about this before, but I'd never heard of you." That is also why we attempt to attend Netherlands-related events in North America whenever possible. They generally draw people who have an interest in the country and its culture. By handing out complimentary copies at those types of events we try to raise awareness and hopefully gain regular readers.

Labor Day weekend I was in Tillsonburg, Ontario for a Friesian horse event – attended by at least three hundred people, where I heard no other languages than Dutch and Friesian. Then someone told me that there was another event going on nearby that also had a Dutch flavor: tractor skill games. I headed over and found a farmer's field with at least another three hundred exclusively Dutch-speaking spectators and participants watching people maneuvering tractors to perform tasks like popping balloons, balancing on a teeter-totter and piercing rings. To the casual observer, there was nothing particularly Dutch about the event. Until one noticed the agribusiness booths that were all owned by people with Dutch last names and the food concession which sold croquettes, frikandels (fried sausages) and stroopwafels.

Between approximately 1990 and 2005, groups of Dutch farmers emigrated to find more space and opportunities outside Holland. Alberta and certain parts of Ontario were among the most common destinations. When we packed our bags in 1999, the international mover who came for a quote asked us what the destination was. "Penticton, British Columbia," we said. He had no idea where that was. "If you were going to some major destination like Toronto, Calgary or Lacombe, I'd know where it was."

"Lacombe?" I asked. I'd never heard of the place.

"Oh yes, we have at least two families a week moving to Lacombe." The influx of Dutch farm families has rekindled and reinvigorated Dutch-related institutions in Ontario and Alberta and gives rise to new ones. Dutch amateur dramatics in Ontario, speed skating in Alberta, and Friesian horse events in both provinces come to mind.

Most of the people at the Friesian horse and tractor skills events represented the latest group of Dutch immigrants to North America, with between fifteen and twenty-five years under their belts.

That is a far cry from the group that approached our regular contributor Alison Netsel to ask her to speak at their annual event: *The Holland Society of New York*. Unfortunately, Alison could not make it over from Europe, and I offered to step in. And thus I gave a presentation to members of one of the most exclusive clubs in the country. To be admitted, you must prove that you descend in the male line from someone who lived in New Netherland prior to 1675. The Quackenbushes, Van Voorhises, Van Buskirks and Bogarts have more than 350 years on the farmers of Tillsonburg and Lacombe. But they have enough interest in their history to organize, and reach out to *DUTCH, the magazine*. And that is what we like to do with the magazine: reach that widely diverse diaspora of Dutch settlers and their descendants with topics that are of general interest to anyone who is interested in Dutch culture, traditions, history and society, and in the presence of the Dutch in North America, whether they arrived with Adriaen Block in 1613, with the Reverend van

Raalte, the founder of Holland, Michigan in 1847, on the *Groote Beer* in 1952, or by *KLM* in 2013.

November/December 2019

The King and Queen Visit Toronto

King Willem-Alexander and Queen Máxima of the Netherlands came to Canada in late May and the USA in early June 2015. The royals came to Canada for a state visit. In the USA their sojourn was billed as a less prestigious official visit. Diplomatic protocol prescribes what is required during a state visit, including a twenty-one-gun salute, an official state banquet hosted by the country's head of state, and other trimmings. An official visit is a much less formal affair. The President of the United States is too busy these days to host too many foreign leaders with all the pomp and circumstance that true state visits demand. So those are limited to the major world players. It was generally considered a significant coup for the Dutch diplomatic mission in Washington that they had managed to get the king and queen a fifteen-minute private meeting with the president. When the president let it run late by five minutes and gave his visitors twenty, that was widely regarded as a very special gesture showing significant goodwill to his visitors. An occasion like that sure helps put the relative importance of your own country and its monarch on the world stage into perspective.

That perspective was hard to find in the run up to the state visit to Canada. The announcement in February that the Dutch king and queen were coming to Toronto had thrown the local Dutch community and the diplomatic representatives in Ontario (the Ambassador in Ottawa, the Consul-General in Toronto and their respective teams) into a wild frenzy. The biggest question for many of the 500,000 Dutch-Ontarians was whether they would get to see, possibly even meet, the king and queen.

When it was announced that there would be an official reception for the Dutch-Canadian community in the *Art Gallery of Ontario* and that there would be room for about two hundred people, I wondered how those two hundred would be selected. The Consulate General quickly announced that except for a handful of WWII veterans, all the spots would be filled by lot. A wise decision. No preferential treatment for the leaders of Dutch social clubs, influential businesspeople, chairs of charities, or publishers of Dutch magazines!

That would eliminate the need for the consulate to decide which 0.04 percent of the Dutch community was worthy of an invite – obviously, an impossible task. Besides, a handpicked approach would probably favor the self-important and the pushy over the truly deserving. So a lottery with very long odds it would be. At least, depending on how many online registrations were received, and that of course we don't know. What we do know is that my wife Petra and I were among the four hundred or so (the numbers had been boosted) lucky winners of an invitation and that many leaders of Dutch clubs, influential business people and chairs of charities were there too!

The question remained whether there would be an opportunity for the general public to greet the royals. It took quite a while before it was announced that after a brief visit with the Premier of Ontario at the Legislative Assembly at Queens Park in Toronto, the king and queen would take a little walk along the grounds towards the next stop on their busy itinerary, an 'innovation hub' or something trendy like that.

I had applied for accreditation for some of the local events and made my way over to Queens Park at about 8:30 a.m. to pick up my credentials for the 11:00 a.m. visit and to talk to the assembled crowd of well-wishers. There were about a dozen people waiting, some of whom had left home very early in the morning to secure a prime spot. They expressed their surprise at the low turn-out. I admitted I was surprised too. Especially because it promised to be a gloriously beautiful day. I left the royalty fans to join the rest of the press corps at the side entrance where the Lieutenant-Governor of Ontario awaited the king and queen, who soon arrived in a shiny black *Lincoln Town Car*. After a cordial greeting the royal couple were ushered up the steps into Queens Park to sign the guest book and have a private meeting with the premier, Kathleen Wynne. Wynne greeted the royal couple in fluent Dutch, which she learned while she lived in the Netherlands for three years in the late 1970s. When Wynne and the royals withdrew into a private room for a brief conversation, I went outside with the rest of the press.

The crowd had grown to around eighty. I noticed a group of approximately twenty middle-school-aged children waving little Dutch flags. I went over and asked them if they had a special relationship with Holland. "Oh, Holland? Where is that? We're visiting the Legislative Assembly for our civics class. They told us there is a real king and queen in there. Is that true?"

There was an advantage to the crowd being so small. Virtually everyone got to personally shake the hand of the king or queen (they walked down the wide path in front of the building on opposite sides). The couple were very gracious and took their time for a brief chat here and there. The queen blew a kiss to a little girl in a wheelchair, the king laughed boisterously, and I took a selfie with the royal couple behind me. I said "your majesty" as they walked past and the king turned his body toward me as if I had pushed a special button, he grabbed my hand and shook it. A performance he got to repeat later that day at the reception. I don't think he remembered me from the morning as he said after Petra and I had been announced: "I am very pleased to meet you, Mr. Bijvoet."

As the king and queen continued their walk along a barrierless path that was lined by Torontonians on their lunch break who had wandered over to see what all the commotion was about, the security detail, both Dutch and Canadian, got visibly tense. It was clear that they did not like this at all. The king and queen, however, seemed to thoroughly enjoy their casual mingle with the crowd.

The king noticed a man on the sidewalk selling Dutch flags and soccer paraphernalia. He walked over, shook the man's hand, and said to his wife, laughing boisterously again: "This man is the best entrepreneur in Toronto."

And then the security detail had had enough. They piloted the king and queen into the invite-only event at the innovation center and sighed a sigh of relief.

The visit to Toronto had come and gone, an event of significant importance to the local Dutch community, which went by virtually unnoticed to the Canadian public at large. Very few of our Canadian friends were even aware of the visit, which commanded a tiny number of column inches deep inside the local newspapers and less than a minute in newscasts on radio and TV. But for us it was lots of fun.

September/October 2015

Family Vacation

In November and December, I spent three weeks in the Netherlands with the family. It was the first time in six years that we had visited with the entire family, and it was interesting to see the country through their eyes. I visit on business trips, but a family vacation gives a different perspective. Overall the unsurprising conclusion is that some things are better there, some are better here, some are different but not necessarily better one way or the other, and some are simply the same. As my daughter summed it up neatly when she told her class about the trip: "You get free coffee in supermarkets, but you have to pay to pee."

My children know they are ethnically Dutch, of course. How can you miss that fact if your dad publishes a magazine called, well, *DUTCH*. They identify strongly with their heritage, although three of the four were born in Canada and the first was thirteen months old when we got here. School projects will invariably be about Holland, and there is no question about which team they support come *FIFA World Cup* time. All four of them speak very passable Dutch, and they had no problem making themselves understood in the Netherlands. To my big surprise, no one tried to speak English to them. In the past, I noticed a significant level of enthusiasm by Dutch people to try their English language skills out on Anglophones, often to the chagrin of the poor expatriate Englishman, American or Canadian desperately trying to learn and practice Dutch. Maybe it is a testament to my children's proficiency, I may venture, as a proud father.

What else did they find remarkable? That cycling is a mode of transportation and not a sport. We rented bikes and stopped to have a brief family discussion about where to go next. A friendly passer-by mistook our little planning exercise for confusion over our route and kindly enquired where we wanted to go so he could give us directions. When we told him we were just touring without purpose, he seemed confused. And that in turn confused one of my kids, until the penny dropped: "Oh, the Dutch bike to go somewhere. We bike as exercise."

My oldest daughter remarked upon her discovery that quaint, old Dutch houses are everywhere. I was surprised at her surprise. What else did she expect? She had thought that vintage Dutch houses would be a rarity in real life, like wooden shoes, or like igloos and teepees in Canada. But after walking and cycling through the centers of Amsterdam, Haarlem, Amersfoort, Leeuwarden, Utrecht, Zwolle and sundry smaller towns and villages, she could only conclude that historic houses are everywhere. She loved it.

For my wife Petra and me the experience was based not only on a comparison between 'here' and 'there', but also of course between 'then' and 'now'. Has Holland changed since we last lived there? Of course, it has. It has been seventeen years after all. But significantly? Not really. On the one hand, convenience and liberalization have slowly crept into the opening hours of businesses and shops. Grocery stores do not adhere to the very strict times that they did in the past, and Sunday opening is common, although nowhere near universal. On the other hand, service delivery outside of regular hours still seemed quite rigid elsewhere. We could, for example, only check in to our cabin in a bungalow park on either a Monday or a Friday and then only between 3 p.m. and 8 p.m. When we expressed our surprise at this to friends they said: "Oh yes, that's normal. It's the same everywhere."

A full analysis of what we witnessed and experienced during our trip could fill many pages. But in the end as my daughter noted, returning to coffee to explain how Canada and Holland are different: "You don't get refills, but you do get a cookie." She did not know what was better, although I think she leaned toward the cookie.

March/April 2017

The new DPs

After its annual Sinterklaas celebration, I had a long conversation with a member of the *Dutch-Canadian Association of Toronto*. He is in his mid-eighties, and I asked him about the circumstances of his emigration to Canada in the early 1950s. He was very frank about his experiences. He and his wife had a very tough time. They left Holland almost on a whim. There was no work for him in the Netherlands and nowhere to live. Only three weeks passed between the decision to leave and departure.

Emigration was the default option for many young Netherlanders between 1947 and around 1964. The country was reeling from war and occupation, its industry destroyed, and its housing stock devastated. Families cramped into tiny apartments; three, four generations together. The Dutch government actively stimulated emigration to the point of subsidizing it from the early 1950s onward.

Conversely, Canada welcomed the newcomers. It needed people to fill the sparsely populated land, as it still does. Canada was not the only destination, although it was the most popular one. Many went to the USA, Australia, New Zealand, South Africa, Brazil, and for Jewish emigrants, there was also Israel. In all those countries there are still Dutch retirement homes, for what is probably the last cohort of the mass departure of the post-war years.

It is hard to imagine now, sixty to seventy years later, but overall about five percent of the post-war Dutch population (one in twenty people) left the country. In 1953 more than 25,000 Dutch arrived in Canada. These days it is around three hundred per annum.

Over the years many individual stories have been told. On the whole it is not unfair to say that these stories emphasized success. They may have started with hardship, but all the more shining the eventual triumph over adversity. And it is de rigueur to conclude: we are glad we came to Canada, the USA, Australia. There is no doubt, many immigrants, the majority probably, were successful, depending of course on which yardstick you use to measure success. However, there are also many examples of people who look back and if they are honest with themselves say: why? Why did we do it? Are we really better off than if we had stayed? Was an entire life of homesickness worth it?

The gentleman I spoke to arrived in Canada, twenty-three years old, his wife even younger, unskilled, without speaking a word of English. The Canadians considered him a DP ('Displaced Person'), in current terminology, a refugee. (Unlike many of the German and East European immigrants, the Dutch were not truly DPs. And they resented the label. But how were the Canadians supposed to know the difference?) Through a well-meaning acquaintance he got a job for which he truly was unqualified. He lost it after two weeks. His wife got pregnant, and there was no money. Not even for a hospital visit in pre-universal-healthcare Canada. Did he ever consider returning to Holland, I asked him. "We would have returned in a heartbeat," he said, "but we could not afford the journey." His story, as I have found in talking to immigrants since I first got involved with *De Krant* in the early 2000s, is not unique. It may not be the norm, but it is certainly not the exception either.

How different things are now. A friend of ours, three years in Canada on a temporary work visa, always swore that it was for the experience, that she would return to Holland after three years. But she likes it here. And she might want to stay. She speaks good English, is well-educated and does have a choice. But sometimes having a choice is hard. So she took her two children with her on the plane to Holland to settle the matter once and for all. But as I expected, the trip only increased her uncertainty. Canada has many advantages, but so has Holland. What to do? And how not to forever second-guess your decision, whatever it turns out to be.

However big the difference between the experiences and opportunities, one thing remains for both generations of immigrants: once you have made the leap, you are forever doomed to live life with two identities, two loyalties. Rationally you can choose, but emotionally you are trapped. Some part of you always remains in the place where you did not stay.

And where the hardship for the generation of the fifties came early in life, I wonder, will ours come toward the end? By the time we can no longer travel, when we fall back into the language and culture of our youth, the institutions founded by the immigrant throngs of the 50s will no longer exist. There will be no more Dutch retirement homes in Canada, no Dutch clubs, no Dutch stores, no Dutch credit unions, and no Sinterklaas parties. In our old age, we may well be the DPs.

January/February 2016

EXPLORATION

Jersey Dutch

L ike animal and plant species, languages are becoming extinct at an alarming rate. Although we cannot blame that on climate change, the trappings of modern society are clearly responsible. Globalization of communications, ever increasing international trade volumes and worldwide mobility of people have made English the undisputed lingua franca of the modern world. The widespread use of a truly global language espoused by the creators of artificial tongues such as Esperanto and Volapük seems closer than ever. The only thing is ... the idealists wanted a neutral language that would give no one an unfair advantage because they were native speakers, or affiliated with a particular country or region. After all, as Yiddish linguist Max Weinreich famously remarked: "A language is a dialect with an army and a navy."

Approximately once every three months, somewhere in the world, a language becomes extinct – and quite literally, that means that the last speaker of that language dies. Because most of these languages are practically undocumented, we can only feel sad that another unique form of expression and world view is lost forever. Even though we should appreciate the positive aspects of the convergence of the world on a single language for the purpose of international communications, we can't help but mourn the death of an entire culture that is embedded in a language. Many bemoan the 'Americanization' of world culture as being at the root of this decline in linguistic diversity. And there is some truth in that.

Languages are vulnerable. If all the native speakers of a language stop teaching it to their children (for whatever reason – economic expediency, political pressure, autocratic dictate), a language can become extinct in a single generation. Look for instance at the Dutch Reformed communities that sprung up in Canada in the 1950s as a result of the big post-war emigration wave. We see that a very conscious effort was made by their leaders to create faith-based communities and institutions, including schools, colleges, retirement homes, newspapers, labor unions, youth clubs, credit unions and so on, coupled with an equally conscious decision to let go of the Dutch language in worship as well as in public and private life. Yet, as is the case for example among Mennonites, Orthodox Jews, or the Amish, where the ancestral language survived, a decision could have been made to preserve Dutch as a viable distinguishing group language. As we know, however, it did not. Yet that is not inevitable.

Languages can also be extremely resilient. Until surprisingly recently, some, now alas extinct, native varieties of Dutch were spoken in the eastern United States. It can almost be said that the Jersey Dutch and Albany Dutch dialects (no army and navy, remember) go against all that has been said in the first few paragraphs of this article. If there is any place in the world where one would expect 'Americanization' to have taken firm root, it would be within twenty or thirty miles of Wall Street. Yet it is exactly there that until well into the 20th century people still spoke a foreign dialect that had been brought to America more than three hundred years earlier.

New Netherland, centered on Manhattan, New Jersey and the Hudson Valley, was a Dutch possession for a mere half century, but Dutch, despite the onslaught of English, remained the predominant language of the region for a remarkably long time. In some areas it was the only language spoken widely until the American Revolution, and it was only after 1776 that the language was gradually displaced almost everywhere by English.

The other remarkable thing (in comparison to more recent practices as mentioned above) is that it was exactly the allegiance to the Dutch Reformed faith that acted as a conserving influence, rather than as an agent of change. Theodore Roosevelt, who was born in New York City in 1858, remembered that his grandfather's church had still used Dutch exclusively in its services, although all he knew in Dutch was a nursery rhyme 'Trippe Trappe Troontjes' that his grandfather had taught him. A church in Kingston, in the Hudson Valley, used Dutch in its services for the last time in 1809 – some 160 years after it had been established.

It is not surprising that the Dutch language would give way in New York City first, where the Industrial Revolution and the influx of new immigrants made itself felt much more than in the countryside around Albany and in northern New Jersey. There, Dutch remained the common language in the villages, where social life centered on a Dutch church and an associated Dutch school, for several more generations.

The eighth president of the United States, Martin van Buren, had the distinction of being the first president to have been born a US citizen, but he was also the first, and thus far the only, president whose native language was not English. He was born in 1782 in Kinderhook, New York, twenty-five miles south of Albany, a tight-knit Dutch community. He continued to speak Dutch with his wife Hannah Hoes until she died. Both Van Buren and his wife are reputed to have had a marked Dutch accent. (For more on Van Buren and Kinderhook, see page 63.)

As the Dutch language became more isolated in smaller rural pockets, its decline accelerated. Where Van Buren, and Theodore Roosevelt's grandfather Cornelius, who were contemporaries, still spoke Dutch, their grandchildren had all but lost the language. And so Dutch became increasingly the language of the elderly and the remote. The Dutch speakers of New Jersey, in particular the rural counties of Passaic and Bergen, were cut off from those in the countryside around Albany. Two distinct dialects, which had already been emerging over time, grew farther apart and gave us the terms Jersey Dutch and Albany Dutch. A distinct variant was spoken until at least the 1930s by the Ramapough Mountain Indians. They were recognized as a Native American tribe by the state of New Jersey in 1980, although the federal government has not extended its recognition to the group. The Ramapough are said to be of Dutch, African American and Native American ancestry, but because of their desire to become a federally recognized tribe, they have been reluctant to acknowledge that mixed origin. Tribe members carry clearly Dutch sounding names such as Van Dunk, De Groat and De Freece.

So when did Albany Dutch and Jersey Dutch become extinct? In 1921 H.L. Mencken wrote in his seminal work *The American Language*: 'Jersey, or Bergen County Dutch, [..] is spoken by the descendants of seventeenth century Dutch settlers in Bergen and Passaic counties, New Jersey. In New York, as everyone knows, Dutch completely disappeared many years ago, but in these Jersey counties it still survives, though apparently obsolescent, and is spoken by many persons who are not of Dutch blood, including a few negroes.' Interestingly, he also goes on to quote a 1910 study on the language, which notes that these descendants of the original Dutch settlers did not mingle with the recent influx of new immigrants to Paterson, the county seat of neighboring Passaic County, although this is contradicted by Jacob van Hinte in his 1922 book *Netherlanders in America*.

In 1958, William Z. Shetter of the University of Wisconsin wrote in the linguistic journal *American Speech*: 'The Dutch of seventeenth-century New Netherland seems only in the last dozen years or so to have become finally a matter of the past.' One of the last speakers of Jersey Dutch, J.B.H. Storms, was interviewed extensively in 1938 and 1941, and some field notes were made about his recollection of the language. Unfortunately, no one seems to have had the foresight (or possibly the means) to record Storms, who was eighty years old in 1941. We don't know how fluent Storms was, nor whether he had spoken Jersey Dutch daily in his early years, or whether he just recalled snippets of how his elders had spoken it. Yet, based on the detail of information he gave, it appears that he did have an extensive command of the language.

Based on the 1910, 1938 and 1941 descriptions, several distinct features become apparent. Jersey Dutch vocabulary had been influenced by English – although it is not clear to what extent this may have been idiosyncratic usage by Storms after decades of speaking mainly English – and had also retained some archaic Dutch words. Other words had undergone a semantic shift, for example Dutch 'touw' (rope) had changed in meaning to 'reins', and 'vallei' (valley) to 'meadow'. It is also interesting to note that, as with Afrikaans, Jersey Dutch had lost the distinction between the masculine/feminine and neutral definite articles 'de' and 'het', and that all nouns took 'de'. An extensive vowel shift seems to have taken place, for example from 'i' to 'e' so that 'schil' (peel) became 'schel' and 'e' to 'ae', so 'zes' (six) became 'zaes'. Another, more remarkable, change, likely under the influence of English, was that final consonants could be voiced, whereas in Dutch they are always unvoiced. So words such as 'vijf' (five), 'pad' (toad) and 'kaas' (cheese) would have a voiced final consonant, which is consistent with their usage in plural: 'vijven', 'padden' and 'kazen'.

One wonders … if only we had that elusive recording. Is it possible that this extinct language has left some traces, somewhere? An accidental couple of sentences on an otherwise unrelated recording made in the 1940s or 50s? Or is there an octogenarian somewhere in Bergen County or the Hudson Valley who, like Theodore Roosevelt, remembers a nursery rhyme or a few sentences a grandparent taught them? The last remnants of an otherwise extinct language. If only ...

January/February 2014

Schenectady's Stockade District

Schenectady was the northwesternmost settlement of New Netherland and was strategically located for commerce with the Native American nations of the area. It has a rich and long history, which is intimately intertwined, especially in its first few centuries, with the Dutch settlement of the Hudson and Mohawk River valleys. It also home to one of the best preserved old Dutch neighborhoods in all of former New Netherland.

In 1661 Beverwijck (current day Albany) resident Arendt van Curler purchased a plot of land from the Mohawk Nation on the south side of the Mohawk River. A year after he acquired the land Van Curler, who was born in Nijkerk in the Netherlands, brought a group of fifteen families twenty miles through the dense pine forest from Albany, to found the village of Schenectady, a rendering of the original Mohawk name for the area, which was Skahnéhtati, meaning 'beyond the pine plains'.

Land was allotted to the settlers, who cleared it and built houses and barns. The area was wild frontier land, and for the safety of the villagers a stockade, or palisade (defensive wall of tree trunks) was built around the core of the village. The Dutch settlers were on good terms with the local Mohawk nation, with whom they had a mutually lucrative trading relation, and had signed a treaty as early as 1618. But there was danger from the French to the north and their Huron and Algonquin allies, who had been pitted against the Mohawk fighting the so-called 'Beaver Wars' for decades.

Throughout the first two decades of Schenectady's existence, it remained a small frontier village surrounded by dense pine forests. Bears, wolves, wild turkey, deer and buffalo were regularly seen, even within the stockade. But nevertheless, civic life developed. A crowning achievement was the official establishment of a Reformed Church in the town sometime in the 1670s. The exact date is unknown, and the church itself, which is still flourishing as a congregation, albeit in its sixth building since its founding, has designated 1680 as the date it was organized, simply because that is where the extant list of elders and deacons begins.

In 1690 disaster struck. After the English had taken over New Netherland in 1664, the ongoing struggle for control of the Northeastern sections of the continent between the English and the French directly impacted the Dutch settlers and their Native American neighbors. During King William's war between France and England, in retribution for the sacking of the town of Lachine in New France by Mohawk warriors, an alliance of French and Algonquin fighters descended on Schenectady in the night of February 8th, 1690. They found the gate to the stockade unguarded and ajar. They stealthily entered the village, burnt it to the ground and killed sixty of its inhabitants. Another twenty-seven were taken captive. Some of them were rescued by a Mohawk called Lawrence, who pursued the raiders on their way back to Montreal with the prisoners, where some of the remaining ones were executed.

The initial target of the raid was the much larger town of Albany, but bad weather – that night a severe blizzard raged – prevented the attackers from getting to Albany. One man who made it to Albany was Symon Schermerhorn, who although heavily wounded, rode to Albany to warn its inhabitants and the settlers whose farms he passed along the way of the potential danger posed by the attackers. The memory of Schermerhorn's ride lives on in an annual re-enactment by the mayor of Schenectady.

The city was rebuilt within the boundaries of the old stockade. Many houses were built in the Dutch colonial style and the city retained a distinct Dutch character, with most of its population of Dutch and mixed Dutch-Mohawk heritage until at least the late 1700s. It was not until after the American Revolution that pastors were called to the church that were educated in North

America and not in the Netherlands. When the Reformed Church celebrated its bicentenary in 1880, a service was held in Dutch and in a report on the proceedings contemporary historian Jonathan Pearson wrote: "There were probably as many as one hundred in the audience, mostly elderly people, who understood most of the once familiar language of the church and city".

After the completion of the Erie Canal in 1825, and an influx of New Englanders and other newcomers, Schenectady became an industrial city, home to among others the *Edison* and *American Locomotive (ALCO)* companies. And although many of its inhabitants can still trace their ancestry back to the original Dutch settlers, the city itself became thoroughly Americanized. A process that one of the Reformed Church's most revered pastors, its seventh and the first to have studied for the ministry exclusively in North America, strongly supported. Dr. Dirck Romeyn, pastor from 1784 until 1804 underlined that the people of Schenectady had to realize that they were no longer 'Dutch, English or Scotch, but for all times Americans' but that they could nevertheless 'honor the fathers and the traditions of the past, yet be none the less American Christians'.

Schenectady's Stockade District, still covers essentially the same area as the original stockade of the 17th century. It was listed on the *National Register of Historic Places* in 1973 and the *National Park Service* has described it as having 'the highest concentration of historic period homes in the country', despite an 1819 fire, which destroyed many original Dutch houses. More than 40 of the remaining ones are older than 200 years.

A walk through the Stockade District gives the visitor a good sense of what the village would have looked like in the 18th century. Apart from the old houses, visitors should also take in the 1887 statue to Lawrence, the hero who rescued some of the settlers from the French, and of course the *First Reformed Church of Schenectady*. Although the edifice is relatively new (a 1950s reconstruction of the 1863 fifth church, which burnt to the ground in 1948) inside there are several historical reminders of the original Dutch settlement, including a model of the very first wooden church of the 1670s and a flag of the *Dutch West India Company*, which governed New Netherland until the English takeover.

March/April 2022

Collegiate's Mascot

Collegiate School, located in Manhattan's Upper West Side is an elite private K-12 boys' school. In a recent survey by *Niche,* the leading school ranking company in the US, Collegiate ranked 3rd out of 201 for best all-boys high schools in the country, and 7th out of 2,560 best private K-12 schools. It also ranked in the top 1% among best private high schools, best college prep schools and best high schools for STEM. But Collegiate not only bestows upon its students an exceptional advantage in educational and career prospects, it also confers a unique distinction that no other school in the country can give. Its alumni can claim to have graduated from the oldest school in the United States. Collegiate will be celebrating its 400th anniversary in 2028. An education at Collegiate, unsurprisingly, is not cheap. Current tuition is $57,800 per year for all grades, from Kindergarten to 12th.

Collegiate's history goes back to the early days of the Dutch settlement of Manhattan. It started as the *Reformed Dutch Church*'s school in New Amsterdam, and it has for more than a century played up that heritage in its branding, slogans and mascots. The school's colors are orange and blue, based on William of Orange's 'Prinsenvlag' (Prince's Flag); one of its two mottos is 'Eendracht Maakt Macht' (Unity Makes Strength), the motto of the Dutch Republic; its sports teams are nicknamed 'the Dutchmen'; its yearbook is called 'the Dutchman'; and Pegleg Pete was until last year the sports teams' mascot.

Pegleg Pete was a cartoon version of a Dutch settler with a wooden leg. Similar figures have been used at Collegiate at least since the early 20th century, but the version most alumni know is a caricaturized drawing by Walt Kelly, a cartoonist and animator best known for his syndicated strip *Pogo.* He created the drawing in the 1960s when his two sons attended the school. It is claimed by some that the image is based on Peter Stuyvesant, Director-General of New Netherland from 1647 until 1664, when the British took control over the colony. Although Stuyvesant, like the mascot, had a wooden leg, it has never been firmly established that Kelly based his character on the Director-General; many students over the years thought he was a nameless pirate.

In February 2019 an 'Open Letter to the Collegiate Community' signed by 28 students was printed in the *Collegiate Journal*, the school newspaper. It stated that Collegiate must confront its problems with racism and intolerance. After citing multiple instances of racism, it goes on to ask for nine distinct measures to be taken to make Collegiate a 'more safe, equitable, just, healthy, and inclusive environment for all students'. Number 5 on the list of proposed measures was: 'A serious reevaluation of our school mascot. We suggest a simple removal of the peg leg. Peter Stuyvesant was a vehement anti-Semite and ruled by hate and racism. Although, current students may not be personally offended by the mascot, is this the man we want to represent Collegiate? Do his values align with ours?'

So as so often, the grievance concerns a symbol rather than substance. The open letter states 'Here is one interesting statistic: in 1969, there were two self-identifying Black students in the graduating class. In 2019, there are two self-identifying Black students in the graduating class'. Indeed, that shows little progress in fifty years, but I doubt that changing the school mascot will have a significant impact on that particular statistic. Maybe the reality that there are far fewer African American students that can afford the astronomical tuition fees than white students – who form a vast majority of the school population – is not a result of Pegleg Pete but of an endemic problem in society, that requires a much more far-reaching and structural solution than changing a mascot.

One could argue that the very roots of Collegiate are based in intolerance. The 1628 founding date of the school was arrived at on the basis of a letter by New Amsterdam's first dominie, Johannes Michaelis, who wrote in that year that although he did not think he could convert the adult natives, he taught catechism classes to children and trusted that if he separated them from their parents, they could grow up to be good Christians. Reading this in the light of recent revelations in Canada, a connection with the brutal practices of the *Canadian Residential School System* is quickly made. However, although forced conversion of this nature clearly is something we would consider wrong today, there are substantial differences with the residential schools. In New Amsterdam the children were not moved hundreds of miles away from their community, were not isolated from the rest of society and were not subjected to brutal abuse. However, the aspect of forcible deculturization is present in those early days, prior to the official arrival of the first real schoolmaster in 1633, which until 1985 was considered the official founding date of the school. For that year there is documentary evidence that one Adam Roelantsen was the first schoolmaster of the school that was organized by the Reformed Dutch Church. The school was not officially chartered until 1638, which was also long considered the official date of establishment.

It appears that the 1628 date was adopted chiefly to be able to lay claim to the title of 'oldest school in the USA'. Collegiate neatly outdid the other two institutions that vied for that distinction, *Boston Latin School* and *Harvard College*, which date their establishment to 1635 and 1636 respectively.

After 1638 the history of the school becomes less hazy. It is interesting to note that the school was 'payed for at the public expense to instruct the children of all classes', was co-educational and had a mixed multi-cultural student population. It was also directly governed by the Reformed Church.

Despite the English takeover of New Netherland in 1664, the language of instruction of the school remained Dutch for more than a century, until in 1773 the school began teaching in both Dutch and English. The school closed from 1776 until 1783 during the Revolutionary War, when the British established their headquarters in New York City, which was under martial law and from which many inhabitants had fled. Where the introduction of English was still vehemently opposed by several trustees in the 1760s and 1770s, after the seven-year hiatus it appears that English became the unchallenged language of instruction.

In broad strokes the most notable dates in the history of the school after the Revolutionary War include the following. In 1808 school governance ceased to be a function of the consistory of the Reformed Dutch Church and a separate board of trustees, still appointed by the consistory, was tasked with operating the school and appointing its faculty. In 1887 the school, was named 'The Collegiate Grammar School'. This was also the year when the school became fee-paying. In 1893 Collegiate became a boys-only school. In 1906, when New York was in the midst of a period known as 'Holland Mania' that started in the 1880s and during which a re-evaluation of its Dutch heritage was in vogue, the first yearbook named 'the Dutchman' appeared. In 1940 the ties with the Reformed Church were loosened as the school became an independent educational institution, although the connection with the church remained, through low-cost leases for school facilities on church property and designated seats on the board of trustees for consistory members. In 2015 the ties between the church and the school were severed completely, the school started to pay market rent and the church no longer had an automatic right to board seats. In 2018 after at least a dozen or so locations since the 1620s (or 1630s if one so wishes) Collegiate moved to a dedicated 180,000 square foot 11-story building, on Freedom Place in the Upper West Side. In 2019, as we have seen, a letter was published in the school newspaper pleading for a more inclusive Collegiate.

The letter prompted action. A task force (the History and Symbols Task Force or H&STF) was struck, which reported back in June 2020 with a 407-page report. Among its activities the committee polled 5506 stakeholders, including alumni, staff, parents, and students. It got a 31% response rate to its questionnaire about the school's symbols and not surprisingly, assessment of the mascot was fairly evenly split between proponents of changing and supporters of keeping the mascot. The task force concluded: 'The Walt Kelly version – whether it is Peter Stuyvesant or not – has become a divisive element within our community. The students' "Open Letter" did not create but rather surfaced such feelings, as revealed via the H&STF's Direct Engagement and Survey. The current Mascot caricature is offensive to many within the community with respect to race and disability.'

The H&STF proposed forming a committee to redesign the mascot. The new version was recently unveiled. Its imagery maintains the connection with the school's 17th century founding, but any perceived references to Peter Stuyvesant are gone. It is also much less quirky than the previous version.

We have come a long way as a society as rights and freedoms gradually have been extended to ever more people, and although we may still have long way to go in that respect, we have developed, over a period over several centuries, a language to discuss human rights, equality, and equity. Without those developments the 2019 Open Letter could not have been written. But as society moved one way, toward a more inclusive ideal, did Collegiate not gradually drift in the opposite direction? It is worth considering that Collegiate's long and proud history starts with a school that was free, admitted boys and girls, and had a student population that was diverse both in class and cultural background. Collegiate may have made its mascot more inclusive, but that alone is hardly likely to create a 'more safe, equitable, just, healthy, and inclusive environment'. Maybe it would help to look a little harder at how Collegiate's inclusive past could inform its future.

May/June 2022

In the Footsteps
of Martin van Buren

As I drive east down I-90 through upstate New York, somewhere past Utica I see a road sign that directs tourists toward a historic 'Dutch Barn'. It is the first indication that I am approaching my destination: the historic New Netherland settlement of the Upper Hudson Valley. The next is an exit for the town of Fonda. Whenever a list of notable Americans of Dutch descent is published, Henry, Jane and Peter Fonda figure prominently. Their ancestors were among the first Dutch settlers of upstate New York, where they founded the town of the same name. In short order I pass Amsterdam, and then Rotterdam, as I approach the outskirts of Albany, the state capital. Here Dutch explorer Hendrick Christiaensen built fur-trading post Fort Nassau in 1614, which after it was destroyed by a flood in 1618, was rebuilt as Fort Orange in 1624. By 1654 the area around the fort had developed into a small town. In 1654 it was incorporated as Beverwijck (Beaver District), named for the animal that was the source of the settlement's booming pelt trading economy and probably also as a friendly gesture to the city of the same name in the province of North Holland, 'back home', where many rich Amsterdam merchants had built their country homes. When the English annexed New Netherland in 1664, they renamed the settlement Albany in honor of the Duke of Albany, the future King James II of England. In 1673 the Dutch reconquered the area, and for a few months the town was known as Willemstadt. With the Treaty of Westminster of 1674, which brought an official end to the third Anglo-Dutch War, the colony of New Netherland was handed back to the English. Willemstadt became Albany again, and this time the name stuck.

This is my first visit to what was once New Netherland, outside of New York City. I only have a few days and there is not enough time to visit Albany, so, while I resolve to come back, hopefully soon, I bypass the city on the way to my destination, about twenty miles south: the village of Kinderhook. There I have an appointment with Dawn Olson, park ranger at the *Martin van Buren National Historic Site.*

Although several American presidents have Dutch ancestors, most notably the two Roosevelts of course, Martin van Buren is the only one who was 100% Dutch. In fact, he is the only president who cannot trace any of his ancestry back to the British Isles, a matter of some pride to himself. In his autobiography he wrote: 'My family was from Holland, without a single intermarriage with one of different extraction from the time of arrival of the first emigrant to that of the marriage of my eldest son, embracing a period of over two centuries and including six generations.'

After I exit the freeway, meandering Highway 9 takes me south. I drive into what was until the early 19th century a Dutch enclave, as is evidenced by the several Dutch Reformed churches I pass. It is also striking, after four centuries, how many recognizably Dutch words still adorn signs along the road. Mailboxes bear Dutch family names (Van Allen, Gardenier, Schermerhorn), but most are topographical. Virtually every village, stream or field was named by the Dutch and many roads and lanes that I pass were too. As I travel the country roads of Columbia County over the next few days, this observation is repeated continually. When I cross a creek called 'Moordener Kill' I chuckle when I realize that as a Dutchman who has never visited the area before, I probably have a better sense of the meaning of the names of geographical features than many long-time residents. 'Moordenaar' is Dutch for 'murderer', so I presume the 'Kill' (or creek) was named after a crime committed here during Dutch times. When I get a chance to look it up later, it turns out that the creek was the site of an ambush by Native Americans in 1643, in which eleven Dutch settlers were killed. My destination, Kinderhook, translates to 'children's corner'. It was given its name, or so the story goes, by Henry Hudson when he saw some native children playing in the area as he sailed up the river that now bears his name.

I skip the village on my way to the Van Buren site and see the historic *Luykas van Alen House* (a 17th-century Dutch farm) from the road as I drive past. I'll go back to visit it tomorrow.

The Martin van Buren site, *Lindenwald*, is well sign-posted and easy to find. It situated along the Old Post Road to New York. A milestone by one of its gate houses indicates the distance: 134 FNY (134 miles From New York). The visitor center stocks the few currently available biographies of the president. Visitors who are not up to reading a few hundred pages of political biography can view a twelve-minute video about Van Buren and his political career. Van Buren was a remarkable character and his influence on both the politics of his day and the development of the American political system are much overlooked today. He suffered the fate of most one-term presidents: too short a tenure to make a major impact as president. And there is also the implication of the election defeat: he can't have been all that good if he wasn't re-elected. As is often the case with single-term presidents, events beyond the control of the chief executive did Van Buren in (think of Jimmy Carter and the Iran hostage crisis or Herbert Hoover and the Wall Street Crash of 1929). He was elected in 1837, and two months after he took office the 'Panic of 1837' broke out: a financial crisis which was to continue throughout Van Buren's term of office and which, unsurprisingly but ultimately unjustly, was blamed on the president – a telling contemporary nickname for him was 'Martin van Ruin'. In 1840 he won the nomination for his party again, but he was defeated by Henry Harrison.

I am welcomed to the visitors' center by the park ranger on duty, who pages Dawn Olson. Dawn suggests I join the last public tour of the day, which is being conducted by her colleague Lou Miressi and offers to give me a more in-depth private tour of the house and the estate the following day. That sounds like a good plan, and she escorts me to the side of the big house, which Van Buren purchased in 1839 with the intent to retire there. As we get there, Lou, a retired English teacher from New York City, is embroiled in an involved discussion with one of the tour members, a history professor and author, about the importance of Van Buren's involvement in the *Free Soil Party* and whether he was correct in his stance about the admission of Texas to the union. The discussion is vivid enough to conjure up a picture of how these policies would have shaped mid-19th century discourse. Lou's passion for the subject, which is also evident during his subsequent tour of the historic house, demonstrates an affinity that all the staff of the site seem to have with Van Buren, the man, and the politician. They also all seem to feel that his legacy is undeservedly ignored. Lou clearly explains how Van Buren was instrumental in the founding of both major political parties. As vice president to Andrew Jackson, his predecessor, who is generally viewed as the first *Democratic Party* president, Van Buren stood at the cradle of this party. He also actively enhanced the power of *Tammany Hall*, the Democratic Party Machine in Manhattan that controlled New York politics for more than a century-and-a-half. He ran on a Democratic ticket against the Whigs when he was elected in 1837. A decade later, as the Democrats became entrenched in their support of slavery, he ran as the presidential candidate for the Free Soil Party which opposed the expansion of slavery into the new western territories. The Free Soil Party created a conduit by which Democrats found their way to Lincoln's abolitionist *Republican Party*. So Van Buren had a hand in the formation of both.

Lou also likes to point out how Van Buren's life more or less spans the formation of the United States, its western expansion and consolidation after secession and civil war. Van Buren was born in 1782, just six years after the revolution and during the last year of the Revolutionary War, making him the first president born a US citizen. He died in 1862, the second year of the Civil War.

Van Buren's political rise was rapid, and he is regarded as a master of the political game. Contemporary nicknames 'The Little Magician' and 'The Red Fox of Kinderhook' point not only to his short stature and ginger mane, but also to his ability to create coalitions, broker unexpected compromises and achieve his political goals.

Van Buren's political resume is unsurpassed by any prior or subsequent president. He held all the major offices a US politician can aspire to. He was state senator, governor of New York, US senator and secretary of state, before becoming vice president and subsequently president of the United States. Somewhere along the way, he was also appointed minister (ambassador) to Great Britain, although the senate rejected that appointment. Until the late 19th century, Van Buren's achievements and his pivotal role in the establishment of the American two-party system, were highly regarded. But then his life and work slipped into obscurity. So did the house he purchased during his presidency and in which he died in 1862.

Lindenwald remained in private hands until it was recognized as a national historic site in 1974 and came under control of the *National Park Service*. It served among other things as a tea house, nursing home and antiques shop. Now it has been restored to the state in which it is presumed to have been when Van Buren lived there during his retirement. As Lou takes his visitors through the country house, he points out details and explains which items in the house actually date back to Van Buren's days and which are replicas. But beyond the physical surroundings, Lou conjures up vivid images of life at Lindenwald when the former president lived there. "Imagine the discussions that took place here," Lou says excitedly, as we stand in Van Buren's study.

"Henry Clay could have stood here," he points to a spot in the study, "and Van Buren there, debating ..." I forget which subject Lou suggested they were debating, maybe the *Compromise of 1850* or some other issue, now obscure and long forgotten by the general public, but still important to the development of the USA into what it is today. As the tour comes to its conclusion, I realize that despite the thorough treatment of Van Buren and his politics, very little has been said about his connection with his Dutch-speaking upbringing and his youth in the Dutch village of Kinderhook.

When I ask, Lou confirms that Van Buren was brought up speaking Dutch only and that he probably did not start learning English until he was about eight years old. He suggests I take up the subject with Dawn when I return in the morning. I will ... but first I have to go find my bed-and-breakfast, in the old *Van Schaack House*, on Broad Street – I presume it was once called Breedstraat – where I have been allotted the *Sarah Roosevelt Room*.

Broad Street is a tree-lined road that leads out of the village from the village green, toward the county seat of Hudson, where Martin van Buren had his first law practice. According to its website, many New Netherland luminaries, including Washington Irving, and of course Martin van Buren himself, enjoyed the comforts of the large, white mansion. It was built in 1785 by prosperous lawyer and Kinderhook native, Peter van Schaack. Van Buren's maternal grandmother was a Van Schaack; after 150 years of settlement, most Kinderhook families were related in one way or another. The house reminds me of the mansions erected along the Vecht River in the province of Utrecht by rich Amsterdam merchants in the 17th and 18th centuries, especially since it is flanked on either side by other grand mansions, much like in the Vecht region. On its right is the *James Vanderpoel House*, now owned by the *Columbia County Historical Society*. Because the houses were built about 150 years after the Dutch settled the area, it is unlikely that there is a direct connection. It is just the sort of thing the wealthy of the day liked in Europe and North America, I suppose.

My host, John, sits on the veranda enjoying a coffee as I drive up. He takes me up to the Sarah Roosevelt Room which is dominated by a large four-poster bed. Above the headboard hangs a painting of a Dutch pastoral scene with a windmill, a steeple, a farm laborer's cottage on the side of a stream, and a fisherman in a rowing boat. I think it looks like a late copy or imitation of an old Dutch master, which is confirmed when I Google the painter, a P.M.F van Herwaarden. Judging by the number of his paintings for sale on online auction sites for prices in the range of $50 to $150, he appears to have been quite prolific, if not very talented.

The Sarah Roosevelt Room is named for Peter van Schaack's sister, who married into the Roosevelt family and was Theodore Roosevelt's great-grandmother. The interconnectedness of the old New Netherland families who were so highly influential in New York until about a century ago, continues to intrigue me. I ask John when Van Buren stayed in the house. He shrugs: "He must have visited here at some point. Kinderhook was a small town and both he and Van Schaack were lawyers." A compelling point I suppose, though not quite watertight historically.

I decide to take a walk through the village before dinner. I use a map I picked up at Lindenwald: 'Historic Kinderhook – A Walking Tour'. It lists twenty-two noteworthy sites within the village and a few more, including Van Buren's gravesite and Lindenwald, just outside it. The village is small and the sites all located within easy walking distance of each other. It is a quiet, late summer Friday evening. I stroll the few hundred yards down Broad Street toward the village green, a triangular space on the crossroads of two highways with a bank, a band shell and a statue of Van Buren. He is seated on a park bench, in full Van Buren regalia: boots, waistcoat, fur-lined overcoat and his trademark sideburns. He leans on a cane with one hand and has a newspaper in the other; a country gentleman taking a rest during a leisurely stroll. The sculptor has kindly left an empty space on the bench next to the president, so that visitors can take a picture with him. I sit down and take the obligatory selfie, which makes for a nice Facebook post.

In the band shell the town band from nearby Ghent is setting up for a concert. I stroll down Hudson Street, which runs southeast from the village green toward Van Buren's birth site. The village is friendly. People greet each other as they pass by, walking, strolling the streets. It's almost like being back in Europe. The roads are too windy and unplanned, the houses too old and different from each other to be American. It reminds me of 't Gooi, the affluent region about twenty miles east of Amsterdam where doctors, lawyers and TV personalities make their homes.

But really it feels more English than Dutch. The terrain is too undulating. The vegetation too uncontrolled. Nevertheless, there can be no doubt that this is Dutch country. I peer in the window of a local realtor's office and realize that they're still at it. Karen and Jack VanBuren have several listings of surprisingly cheap houses in the area.

In 1631, Cornelis Maessen first came to New Netherland. He was born in the hamlet of Buurmalsen which belonged to the town of Buren, and he adopted his hometown as his last name, a common practice in those days. As we saw Martin van Buren boasted that the Van Burens went back six generations and two hundred years in the Kinderhook area. He would probably not have been surprised to know that another almost two hundred years after he made that boast, the Van Burens are still around, right in the center of his village.

Across Hudson Street from the realtor's office, sits an old red brick house. It was built in 1812 by Lawrence van Buren, the president's brother. Although it is more than two hundred years old, it looks well-maintained. A perfect country cottage. It's for sale, and not unreasonably priced. I phone home, but soon practicality takes over. Kinderhook is still a good six-hour drive from where we live. And really, although quaint and cute and homey, there's not much to do in Kinderhook, and it's too far from New York City – 134 miles as the milestone by Lindenwald says – to make it a base for visiting there. Pity, imagine *DUTCH the magazine* being headquartered in Kinderhook in the heart of the most Dutch of the original Dutch settlement areas in North America, in the house of Martin van Buren's brother no less. Probably best to pop that bubble before it gets too far away from me.

Although the history and topography of Kinderhook are heavily Dutch, the area itself no longer is. A sense that is confirmed when I cross the road and enter the *Flour and Feed, Grain and Seed etc.* building. It houses the *Friends of Kinderhook Memorial Library*'s bookshop. I ask them if they have anything related to the Dutch history of the area. They frown. Mmm, not something that many people ask for. Nothing in the shop itself, maybe in the storage area in the back. I am accompanied by a friendly volunteer, who takes me to a shed where thousands of books are stored, ordered by subject matter. He points out a couple of shelves. If there's anything, it would be there. I rummage for a few minutes: nothing. Back in the shop we chat a little. Yes, everyone agrees the area has a rich Dutch history. But most of the property in the area these days is owned by people from the city, New York or Boston. Country retreats for weekenders, or retirees. Oh sure, there are old families that can trace their roots back to the days of the Dutch settlement, but they're in a minority now.

One of the volunteers knows that a book was published recently, a kind of guide to old Dutch buildings, he does not know the name and they don't stock it. I show him my copy of Gajus Scheltema and Heleen Westerhuijs's *Exploring Historic Dutch New*

York. That's the one, he says, and he writes down its title and ISBN. The volunteers are very helpful and friendly, however, and tell me that if I want to know more about the Dutch history of Kinderhook I should phone Ruth Piwonka, the village historian. They write her number on a post-it note. I call. No answer. I leave a message.

I leave the bookstore and walk a bit farther down Hudson Street to the place where a historic marker indicates Van Buren's birthplace. His ancestral home, the tavern his father Abraham ran, was torn down sometime in the last century, or even earlier. It was there that young Van Buren was first exposed to political debate. Most Dutch boys in the Kinderhook area at the time grew up on homesteads, which were relatively isolated. Abraham van Buren's inn and tavern was a waystation between New York City and Albany and drew a varied crowd of travelers. It also served as a local gathering place, a courtroom, a polling station, and a meeting house. Its yard was used for auctions and markets. Eager to observe, Martin learned a lot about human nature, making deals and reaching compromises. Life skills he would successfully deploy as one of the nation's first career politicians.

As I peer into the undergrowth, trying to imagine Kinderhook in the late 18th century, with stage coaches and horsemen traveling the Old Post Road, I hear music. The Ghent Town Band has started to play. A patriotic march draws me back to the village green. Martin van Buren on his bench has been joined by a few dozen townsfolk who have brought lawn chairs and have settled in front of the band shell. A night of entertainment in Kinderhook. The old president seems to approve of the way the villagers, his villagers, spend their Friday evenings. I listen to the band for about twenty minutes and then head back to the Van Schaack House. Lots to do in the morning.

Breakfast is served in one of the mansion's downstairs rooms for all the guests at the same time, at the same table. It's fun, a communal meal with strangers. Not a situation you find yourself in often in these individualist times. Yet another throwback to an earlier, more leisurely age. We chat as we share fruit platters, freshly baked goods, and egg tarts. My table companions are a wealth management advisor from Boston (in town for a wedding) and two young women who turn out to be ob-gyn residents from New York City. The wealth management advisor's friend owns property in Kinderhook, although he works in Boston. The doctors-to-be drove up last night for a few days away from the bustle of Manhattan. They have been scouring the Hudson Valley for a weekend retreat, but think Kinderhook, although affordable, may be just a little too far from the city. The fact that I am here to write an article on the Dutch history of the area and on President van Buren surprises all of them. Never connected the dots, or read any of the many roadside historic markers I suppose. No matter, they all wish me luck with my article as I excuse myself to head into the village.

Saturday is farmers' market day. Local produce, apples, blueberries, carrots, corn and cucumbers for sale; probably much like in Van Buren's day. One of the farms represented, *Roxbury Farm*, is located on the National Park Service site, and the land it cultivates used to belong to Van Buren, who farmed it after returning to Kinderhook in his retirement. I can't help but notice a merchant from Watervliet. A placename could hardly sound more Dutch. He happily poses for a picture with his Watervliet banner behind him. I decide to complete my walking tour of the village before heading out to the Luykas van Alen house on my way back to Lindenwald for my private tour with Dawn Olsen. I walk south along Hudson Street past Lawrence van Buren's house. I stop and look at the house again. It has a great yard and outbuildings behind it. It seems like a steal … but no, it's simply not feasible. I turn left onto William Street with three more historic Dutch houses, left on Chatham Avenue back to the village green and then north on Albany Avenue, for the Columbia

County Historical Society in the museum, a few more historic houses and Van Buren's gravesite.

Martin van Buren is interred in the *Kinderhook Reformed Church Cemetery*, about half a mile out of town and a mile from the actual *Kinderhook Reformed Church*. The cemetery is a sizeable field with individual tombstones which appear to have been randomly scattered across it. Van Buren's grave is marked by a small plain stone, with just his initials on top 'M.v.B', next to his wife Hannah's, also simply marked, 'H.v.B'. Just in front of the two graves, a monument to Van Buren has been erected, a pillar about fifteen feet high. At its base a small American flag, of the sort waved by spectators at parades, is planted in the ground. Van Buren in death, as he liked to be in life, is surrounded by his villagers. They have names like Hoes, Van Alstyne, Schermerhorn, Van Vleck. His burial in an unremarkable grave – even the monument is modest in comparison with those for many of the other presidents – is fitting. Van Buren was very much a man of the people. As a young man from a humble background, he decided early in life that one way to rise on the social ladder would be to become a lawyer. He started with a local Kinderhook lawyer as a law clerk when he was fourteen years old. In addition to running errands and attending to the janitorial duties that came with his position, he immersed himself in the readily available law books and became an expert in the procedural particulars of running a legal practice. He went to New York City to article with William Van Ness, a native of Ghent, seven miles from Kinderhook, and an old acquaintance. During his eight-month tenure at Van Ness's Wall Street office, Van Buren was introduced to politics and became interested in pursuing a political career. He also sharpened his legal wit and at the age of twenty he was called to the bar and became an attorney-at-law.

Back in Kinderhook Van Buren started a legal practice with his half-brother James Van Alen. He specialized in land claims for small farmers and tenants against the rich patroons and absentee landlords of the area. He achieved the reputation of being the champion of smallholders as he continued to excel in the legal field. He argued his first case before the State Supreme Court in 1808, when he was only twenty-eight years old. He was, and still is, considered one of the sharpest legal minds of the early United States. But despite that, he never forgot his roots, and therefore it seems entirely appropriate that he is buried in a plain field, among the smallholders he championed and with whom he spoke Dutch throughout his life.

I wonder. Dutch was still the predominant language in the area during van Buren's youth, even if it no longer was when he was buried. Would there be any gravestones in the cemetery inscribed in Dutch? I have seen photographs of stones in Brooklyn and New Jersey with Dutch inscriptions. I have some time on my hands, waiting for the Historical Society to open. The pace is slow here. So I decide, without any indication of whether I'll find anything, to check out the oldest looking graves in the cemetery. I amble around the deserted graveyard reading headstones. A vast majority of them have Dutch names, but I do not find any with Dutch writing on them. The old cemetery in the village would most certainly have had those, but it was dug up when this new cemetery was established in 1817 to allow for more development within the village.

As I head back into town, where the *Columbia County Historical Society Museum and Library* should have opened by now, I keep thinking about the demise of the Dutch language in the area. It happened during Van Buren's lifetime, that much is sure. When he was born in 1782 virtually everyone spoke Dutch, the sermons in the Reformed Church were delivered in Dutch, and presumably, inscriptions on gravestones were in Dutch. When he died in 1863, the language had retreated. It was spoken only by the elderly, in isolated rural pockets. Within the space of a lifetime, the development of the United States and the influx of English speakers to the Upper Hudson Valley wiped out the Dutch language, which had survived in the area for almost two centuries. After I have introduced myself, I discuss my musings about this with the friendly volunteer at the Columbia County Historical Society. He is no specialist in the Dutch history of the area, he admits; there is so much to know about the area.

That makes sense, history did not stop with the demise of Dutch dominance more than two hundred years ago. At least as much time has now passed since then, as between that time and the original Dutch settlement. So like they did in the bookshop the night before, he refers me to Ruth Piwonka, the historian of the Dutch Reformed Church. The historical society volunteer has another good idea. He tells me that the historical society has transcripts of the Reformed Church baptismal and burial records, dating back to the earliest days of the church. He pulls a few binders off a shelf and invites me to leaf through them.

It does not take long to find the exact year when the church records flipped from Dutch to English: 1797. Whether a different clerk took over who could not write Dutch very well, or whether the consistory took the decision, I do not know. But suddenly 'ouders' become 'parents', 'dopen' become 'baptisms' and 'getuigen' become 'witnesses'. It is also interesting to see that the names of the newborn are more often, but certainly not exclusively, recorded in their English form, rather than their Dutch form (Andrew instead of Andreas, Anne instead of Annetje). On the December 15th 1782 page, future president Martin van Buren is recorded with his proper Dutch name 'Maarten'. An error on the ledger page for July 1797 is telling. The column headings read 'Children', 'When Born', 'Parents', 'Ouders'. The clerk who started the page wrote the Dutch word for 'parents' where he should have written 'witnesses', a slip of the pen into the more familiar. A very understandable mistake for anyone living and working in a bilingual environment.

Apart from the library and archives, the Columbia County Historical Society maintains a number of historic houses in the area. One of these I passed on my way into town last night, the Luykas van Alen House. After I am finished with the ledgers, I plan to visit it on my way to Lindenwald.

Before you get to the house from the parking lot, you come upon the *Ichabod Crane Schoolhouse*, named for the chief character in Washington Irving's classic story, *The Legend of Sleepy Hollow*. It is a mid-19th century rural schoolhouse, and it is worth paying a quick visit to its single classroom. The Legend of Sleepy Hollow is set in North Tarrytown, New York – much closer to New York City than Kinderhook. North Tarrytown renamed itself Sleepy Hollow in 1996 to cash in on the renown of Irving's story and the reputation of the area as 'the most haunted place in the world'. Kinderhook lore does not buy into that all too easy explanation. One of the guides at Lindenwald told me off the record that Sleepy Hollow is really based on Kinderhook. As Irving describes Sleepy Hollow, and after my walks through Kinderhook and my imaginary encounters with its historical inhabitants, the description Irving gives for Sleepy Hollow seems to fit the village like a glove: 'From the listless repose of the place, and the peculiar character of its inhabitants, who are descendants from the original Dutch settlers, this sequestered glen has long been known by name of Sleepy Hollow ... A drowsy, dreamy influence seems to hang over the land, and to pervade the very atmosphere.' But then, I have not visited Sleepy Hollow with its *Old Dutch Church* and Spuyten Duyvil Creek yet. I am sure that it fits Irving's description just as well. It does not really matter. Sleepy Hollow as these things go in fiction, is probably an amalgam of various Dutch villages in New York state. Irving lived (and is buried) in Sleepy Hollow, but he also spent time in Kinderhook on numerous visits, and The Legend of Sleepy Hollow was first published in a collection of stories, which also includes the famous Rip van Winkle tale, called *The Sketch Book of Geoffrey Crayon, Gent.* Yes Gent, or Ghent of the Ghent town band which plays in the Kinderhook band shell and the birthplace of Martin van Buren's mentor William Van Ness. Anyway, one thing that is commonly agreed upon is that Ichabod Crane is based on Irving's friend Jesse Merwin who was the Kinderhook school teacher, and the Van Tassel family, which features prominently in the story, is based on the Van Alen family. Yes, the Van Alen family which built the Luykas van Alen house around 1737.

It is a short walk up an incline from the little school to the Van Alen house. I walk around it, note the wall anchors, the brickwork, the shutter and especially the Dutch doors, split in the middle, so that the top can be opened to air the house while keeping small children in and animals out. So archetypically Dutch are these types of doors that they are very prevalent in 17th-century genre painting and that both my parental house in Loenen aan de Vecht and the last house that I lived in in Holland, in Abcoude, had one. I am greeted by Danny, the volunteer guide who lives across the street. I ask him if he is of Dutch descent. No, he isn't, but he is interested in the history of the area. He started the day before, so his tour through the house is guided mainly by the written notes he has in his hands. That's okay, he is learning, and all the pertinent information is in his documentation. He points out special features as he reads his notes out oud. Inside, the open fireplaces clearly point to the Dutch origin of the building. Conducive to burning peat, for which the open sides offer ventilation, these types of fireplaces are far from ideal for burning wood, because smoke blows into the house. It attests to how long traditional ways were maintained in New Netherland. A hundred years after burning wood exclusively, fireplaces were still being built in a style suited to the fuel of the old country, which probably no one except the local dominie had ever visited.

The house was extensively restored after the Van Alen family, who had passed it down through the generations, donated it to the Columbia County Historical Society in 1964. The Van Alen family was one of the richest in Kinderhook when the house was built. It is a nice illustration of how wealthy citizens of the day lived. The original consisted of just two rooms, a third was added around 1750. The hub of the household was the kitchen, where life's main business took place. The kitchen was where the family cooked, ate, did their daily chores and slept. Next to the kitchen is a 'best room' or parlor, used for entertaining guests, and for holidays and special occasions. In it a family's prized possessions would be on display, including portraits of the family and paintings, porcelain, and tapestry. The tradition of keeping one room aside for this purpose is one that I remember well from my own youth. Although we did not have one in our house, many of my schoolmates' families did. The room was usually called the 'mooie kamer' or 'beautiful room' and kept locked during the week. It would be opened only on Sundays after church and for very special visitors such as the parish priest in Catholic households or elders and deacons in Protestant ones. Sunday dinner would be eaten there, weekday dinner was generally still eaten in the kitchen, and it was only on rare occasions that I was ever allowed into one of those sanctuaries.

When we are inside, I look at the fireplace and note the Delft Blue tiles around them. They look too new to be original, but they draw my attention because they depict traditional Dutch children's games and some of the toys I see are also on display in Lindenwald. I ask Danny if the tiles are original or replicas. He does not know, understandably, but dives into his documentation and confirms: the tiles were a gift from the Dutch government during the restoration of the house in the 1960s, but are representative of what the originals would have looked like.

The loft which was mainly used for storage contains some interesting artifacts. I am fascinated by the 'senility cradle', a piece of furniture I had never heard of before. It looks like a wooden trough or large rocking cradle and was used in the care of the elderly. I don't particularly like the look of it and shudder to think what it must have been like to be confined to one.

Wandering through the house, I am again struck by the familiarity of it. I grew up in a 17th-century house in the Netherlands, and many of the features are strikingly similar. I thank Danny and wish him luck with his development as a historic tour guide. He thanks me for asking about the tiles, one bit of knowledge he will be able to share without referring to his notes.

I walk over to my car to head out toward Lindenwald, when my cell phone rings. It is Ruth Piwonka. She apologizes for missing my call, but she was out of town. She would be delighted to talk to me and give me a tour of Dutch Kinderhook. "When?" I ask her. "No time like the present," she says. My appointment at Lindenwald is flexible, and I take Ruth up on her offer. We decide to meet in front of the Reformed Church on Broad Street. Do I know where that is? Absolutely I know where that is. I am beginning to figure out the geography of Kinderhook pretty well. Besides, it is across the road from where I'm staying at the Van Schaack house.

The Dutch Reformed Church of Kinderhook is not very old, at least not compared to the many historic houses in the area. It was erected in 1869. But a church, as any member of a congregation will tell you, is not about the building. As the historians of the church write in their introduction to *The Kinderhook Reformed Church – 300 Years of Faith and Community*: '... our venerable brick building with its beautiful sanctuary is indeed a vulnerable and temporal structure. The real church is the people themselves ...' In that sense, the real church in Kinderhook predates even the incorporation of a Reformed Church in the village. As early as 1677, a structure associated with the Reformed tradition was built there. At that time, it was a mission church of the mother church in Albany, served by pastors from Albany and occasionally Schenectady farther up the Hudson-Mohawk watershed (see page 54). In 1712 it was formally organized as a separate church.

The book, published in 2012 to celebrate the Church's tricentenary, lists the names of the members of the first consistory: Jochum van Valkenburgh, Pieter Vosburgh, Laurens van Schayck, Pieter van Buren, Bartholomeus van Valkenburgh and Jan Goes. As I leaf through the book my eye falls on a photograph of the 2012 consistory. And again I am struck by the remarkable continuity of names and traditions in the area. Elder Dawn van Buren and Deacon Barbara Vosburgh carry the family names of two members of the original consistory, after three hundred years. I doubt whether something similarly continuous could be found even in the Netherlands itself.

I am leaning against my parked car as I leaf through the book. A Mini turns into Church Street off Broad Street and pulls over. "You must be Ruth," I say to the driver as she gets out of the car. "And you must be Tom". I apologize for dropping in on her weekend unannounced, but she dismisses the suggestion that this would be a nuisance and brings out a set of keys. After trying three or four of them she finds the right one and opens the door to the church. She takes me inside. I am struck by its size; much too big, I would say, for its current congregation of about a hundred and twenty. Ruth agrees, the congregation has shrunk over the years. She talks about the history of the building, the fourth Kinderhook Reformed Church, which was built after the Third Church dating to 1815, which had stood in the same location, burnt down in 1867. I admire the stained-glass windows, the organ, the well-polished woodwork of the pews and balconies and the calligraphed texts of the Lord's Prayer and the Ten Commandments on the wall.

Ruth tells me about special members of the congregation who have plaques commemorating their extraordinary lives. Cornelius van Alen van Dyck (1818-1895) was a missionary to Syria for fifty-five years, where among other literary endeavors he translated the Bible into Arabic. His translation served as the preferred text for Arab Protestants for more than a century. Tom

Little (1949–2010) was an optometrist from Kinderhook who spent thirty years in Afghanistan. Driven by his strong faith he provided free eye care to the Afghan people. He was killed in the Badakshan Massacre of 2010, in which ten members of an international eye care assistance mission were ambushed as they traveled to Kabul from a remote province, where they had attended to patients. The most renowned member of the church over its more than three centuries of history is of course President Martin van Buren himself. An often-repeated story is that he would lean his head against the wall by his pew, and that over the years a stain developed from the oils on his skin. I ask Ruth to show me the stain, but she kindly points out to me that it has gone up in flames with the rest of the Third Church. Of course. After an extensive tour of the church, Ruth drives me around Kinderhook, pointing out the various historic Dutch houses. As we tour the village we talk about the Dutch history of the area. Ruth, who is not of Dutch descent herself, confirms that the area would have been predominantly Dutch speaking until Van Buren's adolescence. When she drops me off by my car at the church after the impromptu tour, it is finally time for my appointment with Dawn Olson, the park ranger at Lindenwald.

In 1839, the third year of his presidency, Martin van Buren purchased the 137-acre estate with its unassuming brick house, with an eye towards his eventual retirement. That retirement came sooner than he had hoped, when he lost his re-election bid in 1840 to his Whig opponent, William Henry Harrison. He took up residence three months after leaving the White House and began renovating. Van Buren, despite being a man of the people, with sometimes simple desires, also had a taste for luxury and slight ostentation. The walls of the large dining room are adorned with wallpaper that was brought in from Paris and depicts hunting scenes. Dawn tells me that when the house was renovated by the Park Service, they had to go to the same firm in Paris (which still exists) to bring it back to its original state. They managed to match the paper with that used in Van Buren's day. The porcelain has a 'VB' monogram, and there are sizable servants' quarters. I ask Dawn if the bust of Van Buren in the study would have been there during his day, or if it was a later addition. Having a statue of your own head in your study struck me as a little vain. Dawn confirms that the bust would have been there, brought back from the White House. The house, she explains, was restored as much as possible to what it would have looked like during the last decade of Van Buren's life, when he lived there.

In 1844, by which time the previously neglected property had been turned into a successful farm under Van Buren's management, producing all manner of cereals, vegetables, fruits and supporting a sizable menagerie of cows, pigs, sheep, and various types of fowl, he purchased an adjacent forty-acre parcel. In that same year, he ran for the Democratic Party nomination again, but lost narrowly to James K. Polk. He would have one more stab at the presidency. Slavery had been abolished in New York State in 1827, a bill which Van Buren had supported, although he did appear ambivalent toward the issue in his early political career. His father had owned six slaves when he ran the tavern, one of whom, named Tom, was bequeathed to the future president in his father's will. Tom walked away to freedom after three days with the younger Van Buren who did not pursue him. In the 1830s abolition started to gain ground as a political cause. Van Buren straddled the fence; although he had supported abolition in his own state as early as 1817, he did believe in the slaveholding states' rights to determine their own course. However, like many of his contemporaries, he opposed the expansion of slavery into the new western territories. A single-issue party, the Free Soil party, which was comprised of abolitionist Democrats, Whigs and the anti-slavery *Liberty Party*, drafted Van Buren as their presidential candidate in 1848. He received fourteen percent of the vote.

The defeat ended Van Buren's political career, and after one more attempt at the presidency with a different candidate in 1852 the Free Soil Party. But the party did have a lasting legacy: it opened up a route for anti-slavery Democrats to join the new Republican coalition between the Free Soil Party and the Whigs that lay at the root of the formation of the Republican Party in 1854.

Well and truly retired, Martin van Buren returned to Lindenwald and the life of a gentleman farmer. He had lost his wife early, in 1819, and possibly to stave off loneliness and certainly to ensure a legacy, he invited his son Smith to come live with him at Lindenwald with his wife and children. Smith would only agree to the deal, which included inheriting Lindenwald and starting a political career, if the house would be extended and modernized. His father agreed. One of the improvements was the inclusion of indoor plumbing and flush toilets (quite the luxury in the 1840s). Van Buren's *Wedgwood* toilet bowl is pointed out with pride by the park rangers. Well-known architect Richard Upjohn built the extensions to the house, which include a four-story Italianate tower. From its top, Van Buren could check the Old Post Road to see if guests were coming, and inspect his holdings. Visitors are not usually allowed to climb the tower, but Dawn takes me up the winding staircase to its top. It affords a great view of the fields around the estate and Roxbury Farm, which still grows, as in Van Buren's day, produce sold to the villagers of Kinderhook: the Vosburghs and Van Burens, the Van Alstynes and Van Alens. After my tour of the house, Dawn takes me for a long walk around the estate, along the fields and meadows and by the fishponds that Van Buren arranged to be dug. Dawn and I pose for a picture with a cardboard cut-out of the president before I leave to head back to the Van Schaack house for my last night in historic Kinderhook.

The next morning, Sunday, I cross Broad Street to go to the Reformed Church. I had noticed on the sign outside that the pastor is called Rudy Visser. He is also one of the co-authors of the book on the church's history. His Dutch-sounding name intrigues me. Since the incorporation of the church in 1712, thirty-five pastors have been called to serve the congregation. Rudolphus Philippus Visser – as he is referred to in the list of pastors in the book – is the first since 1963 with an indisputably Dutch last name, and the first since 1801 with a Dutch sounding first name. I would love to have a chat. My friendly hosts at the Van Schaack House B&B kept me too long to make it to 9 a.m. Sunday worship, and just as I approach the church the doors open and the congregation pours out. I head on over and introduce myself to the only man in a black suit, who I presume to be the dominie. As I introduce myself and tell him of the purpose of my visit to Kinderhook, he responds with interest and with an accent that only takes me three words to definitively place. He is an Afrikaner.

We both continue our conversation in our respective native tongues, Afrikaans for the reverend and Dutch for me, which are still mutually intelligible. And as we discuss the history of the church and the area, Rev. Visser tells me that when he looks at the list of his predecessors, he feels especially blessed and honored that he was called to serve this congregation with such deep roots in the history of the American reformed tradition. When you go through the list there is even a pastor that was called but never made it to Kinderhook because he perished at sea before he had made it across from Holland. Quite the contrast with the flight from Johannesburg or Cape Town. I am introduced to the Visser family, and he encourages his kids to call me 'oom', literally 'uncle', but in Afrikaans used much more widely as a term of respect for an elder. I am flattered. I ask him if he ever considered that his native tongue may have significant similarities with the language spoken two hundred years before, in the very spot where we stand. Both Afrikaans and the Dutch dialect of Kinderhook descend from early 17th-century Dutch. We know from the scant information that is available that another North

American variety of the language, Jersey Dutch (see page 49), had undergone similar grammatical simplification to Afrikaans, with words losing their inflections and grammatical gender disappearing. We will never know for sure of course, but it almost seems fitting that an Afrikaner, even more so than a Dutchman, is the dominie of Kinderhook. We have an animated chat and I give him a few copies of *DUTCH, the magazine before* I get in my car to drive the six hours back home.

I have literally walked in the footsteps of Martin van Buren, the only American president without a drop of Anglo-Saxon blood in his veins. The only president also who did not grow up speaking English but learned it as a second language. But if that would make him less American in some way, the opposite seems true. He was also the first president to be a 'natural born citizen' of the United States. And as we see over the last few decades that former senators, governors, secretaries of state and vice-presidents vie for the highest post in the land, we should remember that Van Buren filled all those positions during his political career prior to taking the top job. He was instrumental in the institution and consolidation of both of America's political parties. But maybe more even than all those achievements, Van Buren's most lasting legacy may be that that most quintessential of American words, 'okay' was introduced into the language, or at least popularized, because of him. During the election campaign of 1840, Van Buren used the nickname 'Old Kinderhook', abbreviated to O.K. to indicate that a vote for him would be, well, okay. Many conflicting etymologies for the expression have been suggested, but this one is widely accepted by historical linguists as one of the more credible ones.

As I head up toward Albany through the beautiful Hudson Valley, I conclude that Old Kinderhook is indeed OK. And that is a conclusion that Martin van Buren would certainly have endorsed. Despite all his achievements, he was happiest in Kinderhook, among the farmers and smallholders he represented in court early in his career, taking his daily horseback ride and chatting with his neighbors in Dutch. The first paragraph of his will reads 'I Martin van Buren of the Town of Kinderhook, County of Columbia, State of New York, and more recently President of the United States, but for the last and happiest years of my life, a Farmer in my native town, do make and declare the following to be my last Will and Testament ...'

November/December 2015 – May/June 2016

The Dutch Press in North America

The Dutch language was first heard regularly on this continent almost four hundred years ago with the settlement of New Netherland. It laid down deep roots and survived, as we have seen, in spoken form for over two centuries.

Around the same time that Henry Hudson was exploring the North-Eastern part of North America on behalf of the *Dutch East India Company*, back in Europe the very first newspapers started appearing. One of them was the weekly *Courante uyt Italien, Duytslandt, &c.* ('News from Italy, Germany etc.') which started its run in 1618 in Amsterdam, around the same time that the first permanent settlement of New Netherland was established. Many historians consider the Courante the very first newspaper, because it was the first broadsheet and the first to use typographic conventions that are still common in newspapers today, such as separated columns and articles with datelines. Despite the parallel development of newsprint and New Netherland, the colony never did get its own newspaper. We must remember, of course, that the Dutch communities were frontier communities, where the challenge of daily survival took precedence over the latest news from Europe, that education was limited, and literacy low.

The first printing press arrived in the area from Europe in 1685, but it was used mainly to produce books and pamphlets. After a false start with *Publick Occurrences Both Forreign and Domestick* which was intended as a monthly, but was shut down by the British authorities after the first issue, the first regularly published newspaper in the Americas was *The Boston News-Letter*, which started its weekly appearance in 1704. People wanting to read the news in Dutch, were limited to whatever was brought across the ocean from the home country. Note, however, that this did not necessarily mean that the news was much more stale than that in the locally produced English language newspapers. Initially the latter relied heavily upon their counterparts in London as a source for their news.

It required the advent of the next significant wave of Dutch immigration for the first Dutch language newspapers to appear in the Americas. Anywhere where major Dutch settlement took place newspapers were started. The *Sheboygan Nieuwsbode* (Sheboygan Courier) in Sheboygan, Wisconsin, in 1849 was the first of a long list. More than two dozen, sometimes fanciful names remind us of a time when every city and town in the USA and every significant ethnic group within those, supported one or several newspapers. But not many had a lifespan that extended beyond a few years. A few successful newspapers, however, did survive well into the twentieth century. These included *De Telegraaf* (The Telegraph) in Paterson, New Jersey, *Het Oosten* (The East) also in New Jersey, *De Volksvriend* (The People's Friend) in Orange City, Iowa, *Onze Toekomst* (Our Future) in Chicago, *De Grondwet* (The Constitution) in Holland, Michigan, *Pella's Weekblad* (Pella's Weekly) in Pella, Iowa and *De Utah Nederlander* (The Utah Dutchman).

In contrast with the early New Netherland colonists, in this era most Dutch immigrants could read and wanted to stay current with what was happening back in the homeland. Church news and religious backgrounders were important subject matter for these predominantly Christian Reformed publications at a time when theological disputes were commonplace and secessions not unheard of. The longest surviving periodical from this era was not a newspaper, but a religious journal called *De Wachter* ('The Guardian'), which was published in Dutch from 1868 until 1985.

Dutch language newspapers also played a significant role in helping the new immigrants get involved in the civic and political life of their new country, often educating readers in the ways of their new homeland and usually affiliated to a political party. One of the most interesting functions that these newspapers performed was to keep inhabitants of the various Dutch settlements in touch with what was happening elsewhere. Many people moved from one Dutch settlement to another and family and friendship ties between the various communities were strong. So a report on the harvest in a small Dutch colony in Alberta might be read with interest in Pella. The 'correspondents' who wrote those reports often inserted a bit of propaganda for their 'colonie' in their articles, to attract new settlers to their area. Sometimes the tendency to promote one's own colony became so blatant that the newspaper's editor felt he had to intervene. Such was the case when a settler in Alberta bragged about the wonderful climate and claimed that neighboring British Columbia even had a tropical climate, a claim that the editor of De Volksvriend gently refuted, saving face by suggesting that the author meant this figuratively.

It is almost ironic that the last two of these nineteenth century Dutch newspapers, De Volksvriend and Onze Toekomst, disappeared in 1951, just as the third big wave of Dutch immigration was gathering steam. One wonders whether a few more years might have given them a new lease of life. But rather than seeing a continuation of some of the older titles, the new wave of immigrants, which numbered more than 250,000 had to start afresh. This happened soon, mainly in Canada, where the largest number (about 80%) of the new Dutch immigrants settled. The first of these, *De Nederlandse Courant* (The Dutch Newspaper) was launched in 1953 and still appears as an insert in *Maandblad de Krant* (The Newspaper Monthly). It was followed by *Hollandia News* in 1954 and *Good News* in 1958, the latter two eventually merged into the *Windmill Herald*, which folded in 2012. The last of the Dutch language newspapers was started in Vancouver in 1969 as *De Hollandse Krant* (The Hollandish Newspaper), now Maandblad de Krant, or simply *De Krant* (The Newspaper).

These three papers, although they looked similar in their tabloid newsprint formats had very different editorial policies and were complementary. The Windmill Herald was strongly ensconced within the Dutch Reformed Pillar of old, bringing a full page of church news. Apart from that it limited itself almost exclusively to brief news items from the Netherlands. De Nederlandse Courant was more of a community paper for the Dutch-Canadian population in Southern Ontario, reporting on events such as card tournaments, Dutch club meets and consulate receptions. It also printed a selection of news from the Netherlands. Under the 32-year tenure of Gerard Bonekamp (see page 167), De Krant transformed itself from a newspaper to something that more resembles a monthly magazine. Its essays and columns by North American correspondents complement news items, short stories, poetry and verse from the Netherlands.

With the advent of the Internet and the easy availability of news from the Netherlands to anyone who wants it, the reporting function of Dutch language news-oriented publications has fast become obsolete. In addition there are demographic issues. As with the earlier Dutch language newspapers, when the immigration wave that originally created them ebbs away, so its newspapers will probably follow. Their counterparts in other countries with a large postwar Dutch immigrant population have already: De Nederlandse Post (The Dutch Post) in South Africa folded in 2007 and the Dutch Weekly in Australia in 2004, although there The Dutch Courier, a monthly, still seems to be going strong. The last remaining Dutch newspaper in North America might well, now that it has a monopoly position, going on the experience of past immigration waves, survive for another decade or so. But without the unlikely emergence of a large new immigration wave, this publication is also destined to eventually disappear.

As the entire media landscape is undergoing rapid change, so Dutch media in North America change too. Although Dutch news sources from across the ocean are in abundant supply, it seems that the Dutch and their descendants on this side of the ocean have a common bond, something that ties them together and makes them distinct from the former compatriots that stayed behind. And so the desire for separate news outlets geared especially towards the Dutch in North America keeps drawing readers to media to fulfill those needs. Specialized websites and blogs sprung up on the Internet, and like the newspapers in the nineteenth century, often disappeared again soon. Many of these sites cater to special interest groups: expats, aspiring immigrants, second generation Dutch descendants interested in their background, Dutch cooking and so forth. Very popular for almost a decade was now defunct *The Holland Ring*, which had a wealth of information and links and was the most popular Dutch-American portal.

In 2011 the English language bi-monthly *DUTCH, the magazine* was launched, in the belief that with one million Canadians and more than five million Americans of Dutch descent there is a continued interest in a 'Dutch' publication, even if it does appear in English.

Surprisingly, however, the longest lived Dutch language newspaper did not stem from one of the three big Dutch immigration waves. *The Gazette van Detroit* (The Detroit Gazette), started in 1914, published an issue, half in English, half in Dutch, every two weeks until 2018, four years after its 100th birthday. It served the large Flemish population of the Detroit area and was distributed throughout North America.

September/October 2011

A Visit to Lynden

It is just before ten on a mid-December morning as I step out of my motel room. Little droplets float in the air, not quite sure whether they should fall to the earth as thin rain – moth rain (motregen) they say in Holland – or whether they should just hang there in mid-flight as mist or fog. The temperature is mild compared to the harsh winter weather on the other side of the mountains, which I crossed the day before, and feeling the soft moist air is invigorating. Makes you want to get out and do things, work, toil, achieve. I take a deep breath. A sweet earthy smell – a bouquet of berries and fresh mushrooms, a wine buff might say – immediately triggers the synapses in my brain into a comfortable sense of belonging, of feeling at home. I look to my right and above me towers a windmill, not much different from the one at the end of the village street (Dorpsstraat) of Loenen, the town in the Netherlands I grew up in, and to my left, starting at the end of the street, green pastures beyond the edge of the built-up area of town. And when suddenly the church bell chimes the hour, the sensory deception is complete. This is as close as you can get in North America to the Holland of my youth: the early morning bike rides through the dewy air, heavily laden with the surprisingly pleasant, soothing smell of fresh cow manure. Lynden, in Western Washington, a few miles south of the Canadian border, really is just like the Netherlands, partly because the settlers made it so: the church bells, the fields, the windmill. And partly because that is exactly why they settled here: the climate and the land, perfect for dairy farming.

The first Dutch farmers came to the Lynden area in the late 1890s from the town of Oak Harbor on Whidbey Island in the San Juan de Fuca Strait about 50 miles to the southwest, on the Pacific coast. Some twenty-five years earlier, in 1874, Phoebe and

Holden Judson, the first pioneers to settle in the fertile Nooksack Valley near the Indigenous village of Squahalish, founded Lynden. Phoebe had found her 'ideal home', which was, according to the title of her personal memoir (*A Pioneer's Search for an Ideal Home*), what she was looking for. She named the town 'Lynden' after the riverside town in the poem *Hohenlinden* by Scottish poet Thomas Campbell, changing the 'i' to a 'y' for 'esthetic reasons'.

This morning I will be meeting with Ron de Valois, city councilor, volunteer at the *Pioneer Museum* and historian of the *First Christian Reformed Church* in Lynden, which celebrated its centenary in 2000. To celebrate the occasion Ron wrote a book about the history of the church (*Thanking God each time we remember*) – a history that is closely intertwined with the history of the town itself.

I walk down Front Street, Lynden's main downtown drag, from the *Dutch Village Inn*, where I spent the night in the themed *Overijssel Room*. *The Dutch Village*, a covered shopping mall with a little cobblestoned street, a drawbridge across a miniature canal and Dutch facades, was developed in the early 1980s by local entrepreneur Jim Wynstra. It was hugely successful and popular, but now unfortunately stands empty as the new non-Dutch owner seems to be at a loss at how to exploit the Dutch theme and has lost his tenants in the process. Walking through the mall now is a slightly eerie experience. It resembles what a Disneyland attraction must look like at night, after all the visitors have gone home. The inn in the huge windmill which towers over Front Street, another legacy of Jim Wynstra who built it at the same time as the adjoining mall, however, is still going strong. On the main floor is a little souvenir and gift shop, that also stocks sprinkles, rusks and other items that might appeal to a Dutch palate. It is cozy with comfortable chairs and a fireplace. The previous night I had a long chat there with its current owner, Bill, a relative newcomer to Lynden – he arrived in the USA in the late 1940s from Friesland and came to Lynden by way of dairy farms in upstate New York and central California. We speak in a mixture of Dutch and English, shifting languages mid-sentence as a word or phrase feels more natural in one language or the other, until I tell him that I lived in Leeuwarden for a few years. Bill immediately shifts into Friesian, pure Friesian, which seems to sit more comfortably with him than either Dutch or English. The conversation meanders, through war, resistance, liberation and emigration to Lynden and its fertile soil. And its many churches – I note that on the corner of Grover and Sixth I thought I could see five at the same time. The Dutch people of Lynden, newcomers and old-timers both, are pious people. I look at Tammy behind the reception desk, a born and bred Lyndenite, who appears to be following our conversation intently, with a smile on her face. Does she understand Dutch? No, unfortunately not, although she would like to learn it. All she knows in Dutch is that song, you know. "What song?" I ask. "Well, that song that you sing at Christmas time, what's it called again," she asks me. 'We sing lots of songs at Christmas,' I think to myself, '*Silent Night, Oh Come all ye Faithful, Ave Maria* ... well maybe not Ave Maria, these are staunch Dutch Reformed folk who probably do not want much to do with the worship of Mary and popery in general' and then it dawns on me: "*Ere zij God*," I say – the definitive Christmas carol in the Dutch Reformed tradition. "Yes that's it. Ere zij God in den Hoge", says Tammy, "Glory to God in the Highest."

Ron de Valois is a tall, distinguished looking man, with a friendly smile. Despite my pre-announced arrival he is not expecting me, a breakdown in communications somewhere along the line, but he takes the time anyway and we sit, talking for over an hour about Lynden, the First Christian Reformed Church, the Dutch language. After we quickly clear up the mystery of his non-Dutch sounding name – he is of Huguenot stock – he explains that Lynden was never really as Dutch as some other communities in North America, because it was not settled by people straight out of Holland. The first settlers had been in the USA for some time, searching, by trial and error it almost seems, until, as they trusted, the Lord helped them find the right place to farm. They would pick up and start over in different parts of the USA several times in the course of their life. Ron's book lists the charter members of the First Christian Reformed Church. Nine of them came from Oak Harbor, five from the Dutch settlement area in Michigan and one from Nebraska. After the church was organized Dutch settlers flocked to Lynden, mostly to escape the harsh unfavorable climate of the prairies.

"So Dutch was never much spoken in Lynden?" I ask Ron. Well, in the early days church services were held in Dutch, as the settlers clung to the traditions and style of worship of their homeland and they would still speak Dutch among themselves. But the First World War brought changes. The German-sounding language of the Dutch was listened to with growing suspicion by their American neighbors and many younger members of the congregation started to become more proficient in English. In 1918 the first services were held in English and in 1920 the *Second Christian Reformed Church* organized, with services and catechism classes exclusively in English. The language question was a hot topic for another few decades, with one parishioner, as Ron writes in his book, 'not convinced, surely nobody could be a Christian without singing the Dutch psalms'. But, after a transitional period, during which some services were held in English and some in Dutch, English gradually became the natural language of choice. A new influx of Dutch immigrants straight from the old country in the 1940s and 1950s could not change the irreversible decline of the Dutch language and the last sermon was held in Dutch in 1953, simply, Ron tells me, because that was when the last pastor who had a command of the language left. "But you know," says Ron, "when we sing 'Ere zij God,' I still hear a lot of Dutch around me".

We cover a lot of ground starting with the early beginnings of Lynden as a logging town – "but there are no trees," I protest, "not anymore," says Ron with a twinkle in his eye, "the Dutch are hard workers". We discuss the smell of cow manure – 'Dutch Dristan', according to the other, non-Dutch, volunteer at the museum who has joined in the conversation. I learn that four out of eight city councilors, five if you include the mayor, are alumni of *Calvin College* in Grand Rapids. I learn that the First Reformed Church, which did not look that old to me is not the same as the First Christian Reformed Church and I learn that times are changing and that the Christian school is no longer exclusively Reformed, but also accepts members of other denominations. "Even Catholics?" I ask. Even Catholics.

Before I leave there is one last question that I have to ask Ron. The town, that much is obvious, clearly identifies as Dutch, I even see cars with bumper stickers supporting the Dutch national soccer team. On the whole the people of Lynden are devout God-fearing, conservative American Christians. How can they reconcile that with the current image of the Netherlands, with its liberal abortion and euthanasia laws, decriminalized prostitution and drugs, and its overall Godlessness. Ron's answer is simple and enlightening: "I often wonder what happened over there …" he says. And when I stop to think about it that makes a lot of sense. Holland has changed and the descendants of the Dutch in Lynden have stayed much closer to the original model than the descendants of the Dutch in the Netherlands itself.

After I thank Ron for his time, I visit the Museum. So much for planning what I thought would be a quick saunter through a typical small-town museum. Behind the unassuming exterior lies a complete life-size reconstruction of early twentieth century downtown Lynden, the largest collection of horse drawn vehicles west of the Mississippi, a huge collection of model cars, an even bigger collection of agricultural implements and one or two exhibits about the Dutch. As I finally make my way to the exit I mention to Ron that as a city councilor he should do something about the three hour parking zone in front of the Museum. It's not long enough. "They don't ticket there," he says, "but don't tell anyone."

It's way past lunchtime. I would like to sample some of the local delicacies, a good hearty pea soup (erwtensoep) would do me nicely. I have two choices on Front Street: *Dutch Mother's Family Restaurant* with such items on the menu as croquettes and pannekoeken and the *Lynden Dutch Bakery*, with oliebollen, banketstaven (almond sticks) and saucijzenbroodjes (sausage rolls). I walk back and forth a couple of times between the two, less than a block apart, pop into an antiques store and buy a cute little Delftware plate for $1.99 and decide that, dietary considerations notwithstanding, I owe it to my readers to do a little consumer testing and report back on the quality of the green stuff on offer. Both locations offer a nice cozy 'gezellig' Dutch atmosphere and, unsurprisingly, Dutch Mother's is more suited to a sit-down meal, whereas if you prefer a cup of coffee with an almond cookie or a piece of mocha cake, the bakery is your best bet. Both establishments serve a genuine Dutch pea soup. In my opinion Dutch Mother's has a slight edge, its soup being a little thicker, a bit richer than the moderately lighter fare just up the street. But there is no doubt that either of the two will give you a true Dutch culinary experience.

As I leave the Bakery and step back onto Front Street I contemplate the faux facades that some local merchants have put up against their buildings in an attempt to join in the 1980s reinvention of the town as a bit of Holland in Washington State. I'm not sure. The public restrooms with their step gables and the scale model windmill in front them seem a bit, well, a bit fake. I understand the economic motives behind the plans to capitalize on the indisputable Dutch heritage of the city, but somehow I am drawn more to the sturdy squareness of the Bylsma and Dyk buildings, representing hard work, success in a strange land, thrift and unadorned piety: Calvinist buildings, if such things exist. They are much more representative of the true Lynden of the eight decades before the windmills went up. Don't get me wrong, I quite enjoy the open-air-museum-like quality of the signs with 'Postkantoor' (Post Office) and 'Tandarts' (Dentist) on downtown buildings, but considering that the last Dutch speaking dominie left in 1953 it pushes the envelope just a bit.

But never one to prejudge, I decide to do a few more quick checks along Front Street. Amy at the library looks at me with some surprise when I ask her where the Dutch section is. "We don't have a Dutch section," she says. "We have Spanish, Punjabi and Russian sections, though," she says hopefully. But that does not do me much good. I get a similar response at *KATZ! Coffee and Used Books*, a welcoming and well-stocked new and used book store with espresso bar. Sherri – fifth (at least) generation Dutch from Grand Rapids – takes me to the back of the large store, where I get down on my knees to look at the two small shelves of Dutch books. Sherri is happy when I fish out a few German books and a Swedish one, she likes to keep her 'Dutch section' pure. Talking about Dutch heritage and how it is experienced through the generations, she mentions that her son Klayton has a tattoo on his shoulder which celebrates that very heritage. She beckons him and he pulls up the short sleeve of his T-shirt and proudly displays the lion rampant of the Dutch coat of arms and the words 'Ere zij God in den Hoge'. I ask him if his friends have similar tattoos. No, not as far as he knows, he just thought it was neat. The tattoo represents his heritage, his people. "Is it a Dutch thing or a faith thing?" I ask him. "A bit of both," he says.

As my stay comes to a close and I leave Lynden driving north along Guide Meridian toward the Canadian border that strange sense of belonging comes over me again. The long straight roads, the farms with their well-tended front yards, the ditches and the clusters of poplars are a realistic reinvention of the land I grew up in. Only the distant white capped mountains give the game away.

At *Edaleen Dairy*, minivans from Abbotsford in British Columbia just across the line, stock up on large jugs of cheap locally produced wholesome Dutch-American milk. Extended families have come along, kids bribed with a few scoops of Edaleen's award winning ice cream, to make the most of the journey under the strictly enforced Canadian customs limit of $20 worth of dairy per person per trip.

I pass *Ebenezer Christian School*, which celebrated its centenary in 2010, as the sky breaks open and the sun shines through the cloud that has hung over the town of Lynden for most of my stay. I'm driving home for Christmas and as I check that I have my passport handy I find that I am humming a popular tune: 'Ere zij God, ere zij God in den Hoge ...'

March/April 2012

The Comfort Bird
by Hylke Speerstra

It started with an email from Professor Henry Baron of Grand Rapids, Michigan. He wondered if I would be interested in publishing his English translation of a book by Friesian author Hylke Speerstra. He suggested I contact Speerstra myself. I knew of Speerstra, of course. He is the author of a collection of immigrant stories called *Cruel Paradise*, which was also translated by Baron and was first published in 2005.

It is one of the few books (maybe the only book) that captures the Dutch emigrant experience in all its human aspects. Too often, unfortunately, emigrant memoirs are turned into hagiographies or rags-to-riches success stories that leave out the hardships, the intense homesickness, the regret sometimes, and focus predominantly on the positive myth of immigration. In his oral histories, Speerstra tackles the full palette of emotions, the good and the bad. Cruel Paradise is a book that had to be written, but had it not been for Speerstra, it might never have been. It is his interest in the human story and the human experience that drives him. As he said himself: "It has to do with curiosity. If you listen carefully, there are so many human histories that form life lessons. How often doesn't it happen that you are touched deeply by true stories in which reality surpasses fiction? Okay, it is the art – or call it a craft – to record a story in a way that engages, draws in, the reader."

I knew that Speerstra had also published another collection of oral histories, about the experiences of veterans of the Dutch expeditionary force in the post-World War II Dutch East Indies (now Indonesia). It was an unpopular war, and the veterans were reluctant to speak about their time in 'Indië'. The subject carries a special interest for me, because both my father and my uncle were among the 120,000 young Dutch men and boys who were sent to fight a stealthy, cruel guerilla enemy in the tropics. An enemy that, in retrospect, had natural justice, and, of more immediate relevance, American backing on its side. Tricked, lied to, badly taken care of upon their return, and on top of that often pictured as imperialist war criminals, these young men (many of them involuntary conscripts and many of them suffering from lifelong post traumatic stress disorder before the term was even coined) were told to forget what had happened and get on with their lives. Even if they had been willing to relive the trauma of their war experiences in words, no one wanted to listen to their stories. Until Speerstra did.

I was intrigued, to say the least. I phoned Speerstra, and we had an hour-long conversation that covered many topics: Cruel Paradise and the Dutch emigrants, oral history, his admiration for the books of John Steinbeck and Truman Capote, the Indies, farming and, of course, the book that Baron had translated: *The Comfort Bird*, published in Friesian as *De Treastfûgel* in 2011.

We also talked about book publishing. I explained that Mokeham was not really a publisher of books. Our core business at the time was publishing magazines and newspapers. The only books we had ever published were the wartime memories of our readers, *The Dutch in Wartime* book series. I decided to assemble that series because the readers of *De Krant* had been adamant that their stories had to be preserved for their children and grandchildren. I agreed with them, and if I did not publish them, no one would. So we published the series, and I really had no intention of publishing any more books. It is not a lucrative business at the best of times, and it is hard enough work to keep the newspaper and magazine afloat to be diverted from my core business. But Speerstra had a good argument: "If you do not publish this book, no one probably will. The translation is ready. All you have to do is print and sell it. I'll help you. I'll come over to North America to promote it. All I want is for people to read the story." So I acquiesced: "Send me the original, and I'll read it." It was not the first time that someone asked me to publish a book, and it would not be the first time that I turned someone down, I thought.

A few days later, the package arrived. Two books, one in Friesian and the other the Dutch adaptation that Speerstra made himself. I did not have time to dive into it immediately, but when I had to make a cross-Atlantic flight a few weeks later, I packed the Friesian version into my carry-on bag. (I am not Friesian myself, but lived in the capital, Leeuwarden, for three years and decided as a courtesy to the locals to learn the language. I went to night classes and fell in love with the beautiful expressiveness of the language. I never really learned to speak it well, but I read it easily and with pleasure).

I opened the book as we taxied down the runway at *Pearson Airport* in Toronto and started reading. "Your mom has put her head down for the last time," Ytsje Wytsma is six when she hears these words from a neighbor. The children in the village explain to her what that means. 'Your mom is dead.'" Thus begins the story of two families of Friesian farm laborers, which spans three generations. It is based on a true history, and Speerstra has used the original sources and the interviews he had with descendants to write a book that fascinates from start to finish. The visits from flight attendants with a snack or another drink, usually a welcome diversion during a long-haul flight, became pesky interruptions. And by the time we got to Barcelona, I had finished reading De Treastfûgel. I knew this book had to be published, and if I did not do it, it could take the author and translator a long time before they would find someone who would. Not because the book is not worth being published (any editor and publisher will see that this is a fantastic book), but because selling the idea that a translation of a book from a tiny minority language covering the experiences of two farm families from an obscure corner of northwestern Europe makes for a good business decision is a stretch, to say the least. But I like a challenge.

I called Hylke (we had started using first names by this time) when I got back home, and work on publishing the book started. When I met Hylke in Leeuwarden on a trip to the Netherlands, I asked him why particularly this story, of the many he had heard in his eighty-one years. He explained: "Sometimes you run into a story by chance that seems almost unbelievable. It gets stuck in your head, but there's something missing. You don't seem to be able to connect the loose ends. And then suddenly it turns out that across the globe there is a very old witness who experienced the drama himself. That's how I ended up being able to write The Comfort Bird."

That witness 'across the globe' turned out to be a Nanno (Nammen) Hiemstra, dairy farmer and World War II veteran, born in South Dakota and living in Ripon, Wisconsin with his wife, Alice (Aaltsje) neé Coehoorn, born in Iowa.

Nanno was drafted into the U.S. Army after Pearl Harbor and took part in and survived D-Day, where he landed on Utah Beach. He fought his way through France and Germany for another three hundred days, when he had an encounter with his 'counterpart' in the book … Their ancestors came from the same little village in Friesland, Hichtum. His counterpart was a member of the feared German SS-troops. The story makes clear how fate can sometimes determine a life's course.

Hylke interviewed the D-Day veteran in 2010 in Ripon, Wisconsin, where the family had moved from South Dakota for better farmland. Nanno and Alice were in their early nineties at the time but had clear minds and memories. "They were so looking forward to the English-language edition," Hylke told me. But unfortunately, it was given to neither of them to witness its publication. Nanno died in 2015, ninety-five years old, and Alice died in March of 2017, only two months before The Comfort Bird was printed, also ninety-five years old. Alice did live to participate in a celebration to honor her husband, liberator Nanno Hiemstra, in Hichtum in 2013. Several American and Friesian family members attended the service in the eight-hundred-year-old village church.

Nanno Hiemstra's counterpart was Meindert Boorsma, who had fought on the Russian front with the SS. It has taken a long time, but now, more than seventy years after the end of World War II it has become possible to tell a story that is more than the black and white of 'good' versus 'evil' in the war. The decisions made by the Boorsma family are made plausible and understandable in Speerstra's book. A decision may not be right in the light of historical facts, but that may not make it misguided seen in the light of the harsh conditions of the time either.

As we read about the toughness of life in rural Friesland in the late 1800s – agricultural crises and the subsequent adventures of one family through economic depression and dustbowl in North America, and another through political turmoil, ruins, and economic depression in Europe – we realize how much chance decisions and fate determine outcomes across the generations. Speerstra's book is a not just a riveting read, not just a social history of migrant labor and not just a good story. It also gives us insight into what a big impact small decisions by single individuals can have on many lives. And what makes it even more impressive and exciting: it is a true story.

I am proud and honored that Messrs. Baron and Speerstra chose Mokeham to publish The Comfort Bird. It is – and believe me, I am not just saying this because we happen to be the publishers – a book that should be read by anyone who has the slightest interest in Dutch social history, emigration or World War II. And by anyone who likes a good read. Because Hylke Speerstra tells a great story.

July/August 2017

Hylke Speerstra's books The Comfort Bird and Cruel Paradise are available on Mokeham Publishing's dutchthestore.com website and in many on-line bookstores.

Canada's Princess

From May 13th until 17th of 2017, Princess Margriet of the Netherlands visited Canada. The Dutch royal is Princess (former Queen) Beatrix's sister and therefore King Willem-Alexander's aunt. Until the birth of Beatrix's children, she was second in line to the Dutch throne. She has made numerous visits to Canada and is always welcomed with special honors when she comes.

The story of Dutch Princess Margriet's lifelong bond with Canada begins almost two years before her birth, when her mother left the Netherlands during the German invasion in May of 1940. The Dutch dynasty was in bad shape. Queen Wilhelmina, the only surviving child of King Willem III, had only one daughter, Princess Juliana, the heir to the throne. Juliana had married impoverished German nobleman Bernhard of Lippe-Biesterfeld in 1937 after a long quest to find a suitable husband. The marriage had resulted in the birth of two daughters, Beatrix (1938) and Irene (1939). If the Germans were to capture the small royal family and should they not survive the war, it was not clear what the future would hold for the Dutch monarchy. It was not inconceivable that the Dutch would give up on the hereditary rulers of the House of Orange and opt for a republic of whatever nature. There was no clear line of succession, and several distant German relatives could be expected to vie for the Dutch throne. It was not immediately clear if any of these German princes would be acceptable to the Dutch.

So, it was prudent for the princess and her children to leave for the relative safety of England, 'to safeguard the line of succession'. A day after the princess and her family left, it became clear that the Netherlands would be overrun by the German invaders, and within days Queen Wilhelmina also left for England to continue the fight against the Germans, rather than be hauled off to Berlin as a hostage to Hitler.

It was by no means certain in the spring of 1940 that England would remain a safe haven. The *Molotov-Ribbentrop Pact* between the Soviet Union and Nazi Germany was still in force, keeping the Soviet Union out of the war, and there was no indication yet that the United States would join the war effort on the Allied side. The Blitz raged in full force, and London was a dangerous place. A German invasion of the United Kingdom was considered a real likelihood. So it was decided, again for the future of the dynasty, to send Juliana and her children farther away. The Dutch East Indies were briefly considered, but the political situation in Asia was also volatile with Japan's expansionary ambitions, and there was always the risk of anti-colonial unrest among the Indonesians. President Roosevelt had offered refuge to the Dutch royal family, but America's neutrality at the time still posed dangers. Canada seemed to be the best destination: a part of the British Empire, fully participating in the war against the Germans and safe from German raids and invasion across the Atlantic Ocean.

On June 2nd, 1940, a small convoy of three Dutch navy ships which had escaped from the Netherlands during the battle for Holland, stealthily sailed from a small naval base in Southwest Wales. On board one of them were Princess Juliana, her two tiny daughters and a small entourage of adjutants and ladies-in-waiting. The crossing was not without danger. German U-boats were prevalent along the route that the small convoy took to Canada, and a longer, safer southern route was out of the question because of a shortage of fuel. But after nine days, the ships docked safely in Halifax, and a five-year exile in Canada began.

After a brief stay with the Governor General of Canada, the Earl of Athlone and his wife Princess Alice – who, unsurprisingly in the close-knit circle of European royal families, was Princess Juliana's aunt – the royals rented a house in Ottawa. It took a year until Bernhard managed to come over for a visit, and Juliana promptly became pregnant. In those unenlightened days of the middle of the last century, the line of succession to the throne was still determined by gender rather than birth order alone, and should the baby be a boy, he would be the immediate heir to the throne, bypassing even his mother, Princess Juliana, in the line of succession. If the baby were born on Canadian soil, it would become a 'Canadian National' and 'British Subject' and be subject to Canadian law. This would result in unknown consequences and complications and was to be avoided if at all possible. The Canadian government in the spirit of goodwill between the two allies issued a proclamation declaring 'That any place in Canada within which Her Royal Highness the Princess Juliana of the Netherlands may be confined shall, for the period of the lying-in and to the extent of actual occupation for such purpose be extra-territorial, and for such purpose Her Royal Highness the Princess Juliana and any child that may be born shall be accorded immunity from criminal, civil and military jurisdiction whether Dominion or Provincial.' In other words: wherever in Canada Juliana gave birth, that place would be considered extraterritorial, and the baby would not automatically become a Canadian national. The 'place' turned out to be a room in the *Civic Hospital* in Ottawa, where the baby was born on January 19th, 1943. There was some disappointment initially at the birth of yet another girl, but Juliana herself said she was relieved. She feared that the birth of a Prince of Orange and heir to the throne would have caused too much excitement in the Nazi-occupied Netherlands, resulting possibly in spontaneous demonstrations of loyalty to the House of Orange, which would almost certainly be harshly repressed by the Germans.

The baby girl was named 'Margriet', a common Dutch flower of the genus Leucanthemum, known in English as the 'ox-eye daisy' or 'common daisy'. The flower was a symbol of the Dutch resistance, and the intention was to create a deep bond between the Dutch people and the foreign-born princess.

It was not until August 4th, 1945, that the then two-and-a-half-year-old princess would first set foot in her true homeland. Princess Juliana would always remember the hospitality she had received in Canada and said when she left: "Five years is a long time, and one becomes attached. We have made so many friends, we shall leave such happy memories." She also said "My baby will always be a link with Canada. Not only for my own family, but for the Netherlands." And true to her mother's word, Princess Margriet has always felt a strong connection to the land of her birth and has established a reputation as being 'Canada's Princess'.

Nevertheless, it would be twenty-three years before she returned to Canada. In 1967 Margriet married Pieter van Vollenhoven, a fellow alumnus of *Leiden University* where the two had met. Margriet was the first member of her family ever to marry a commoner, and although she had the full support of her mother, the queen, some more conservative members of the royal household took a bit longer to be convinced of the merits of the match. But Mr. (later Professor) van Vollenhoven and Margriet went on to enjoy a long happy marriage, and Van Vollenhoven was fully accepted into the bosom of the royal family. The couple had four sons.

In 1968, it was time for Margriet to return to the land of her birth, to show her new husband where she was born and to reacquaint herself with the area in which she had spent the first two happy years of her life, far from the dangers and deprivations of war-torn Europe.

Full of anticipation, she went to see the villa in Ottawa in which the royal family had lived after her birth, half hoping that seeing it would trigger a memory of her earliest years. But unfortunately, there was no spark of sudden recollection. Another spark did fly. Margriet immediately loved Canada and its people. She returned in 1970 with a visit to the Arctic north, and more than ten visits to Canada followed in the subsequent years.

The princess has always been particularly fond of meeting Canadian veterans, and no visit for her is complete without meeting and thanking veterans of World War II, especially those that took part in the liberation of the Netherlands. This is not surprising if one considers that if it had not been for these brave Canadian soldiers, Margriet may have never seen the land where her mother and older sister were destined to reign as queens. The huge Canadian role in the liberation of the Netherlands and the sacrifices by many Canadians and their families must never be forgotten. And one thing is certain, as long as she can, Princess Margriet will make sure we remember!

As can be imagined, Princess Margriet is always warmly welcomed by the Dutch immigrants to Canada and their descendants. On her most recent visit to Canada, in May, she went to *Holland Christian Homes*, a large retirement complex in Brampton, on the outskirts of Toronto. It was incorporated in 1969 by a group of Christian Reformed Ontarians who had the foresight to realize that the older immigrants would need a place to live in their retirement that fit their heritage and their faith. The first building opened in 1979, and the complex has expanded significantly since. During one of those expansions, in 1983, Princess Margriet was on hand to perform the ground-breaking ceremony. She returned this year to perform the same ceremony for yet another expansion. In her speech to the residents, she said: "I presume that the tenants and residents of today are not the same as the ones thirty years ago! So not many here will remember the previous occasion when we were here for the ground-breaking ceremony for the – then – new nursing home. I cannot promise that I will be back in thirty years for yet another ceremony. My age is no secret as I was born in Ottawa during the Second World War ... The safe and warm refuge Canada provided for my mother, my sisters and myself has had a lasting effect on our relationship with Canada and the Canadians. The decisive role

Canadian soldiers have played in the liberation of the Netherlands is always remembered, especially in the month of May, the month in which the Netherlands were liberated."

She also said: "The ties binding our two countries are strong and lasting, they have grown over time and continue to do so. A tangible token of our gratitude are the tulips that bloom every spring in Ottawa!"

She was referring to the *Canadian Tulip Festival*, which was initiated by Queen Juliana in 1953. The Tulip Festival's website explains its origin: "A princess, whose royal family has been displaced by war, is born in Canada. In gratitude, a gift of Dutch tulips makes its way across the ocean, and the legacy of the Canadian Tulip Festival is created." Over the years Margriet has also become closely associated with the festival, opening it officially in 1995, fifty years after the liberation of Europe and returning again in 2005 for the sixtieth anniversary of the end of World War II.

A qualified nurse with practical field experience, Princess Margriet has been active in the International and Dutch *Red Cross* Societies, chairing various committees. This experience was invaluable when she became the honorary chair of the *Global Health Advisory Board* of Maastricht and McMaster Universities. The two universities partnered in 2010 to provide a Master of Science program in Global Health. Other members of the board include Elizabeth Witmer, the former deputy premier of Ontario and initiator of the proclamation of May as *Dutch Heritage Month* in the Province of Ontario and internationally renowned food safety advocate Mary Heersink. In 2012, Margriet received an honorary doctorate from McMaster for 'her lifelong commitment to international humanitarian causes'.

The bond between Canada and the Netherlands is strong. The legacy of liberation, gratitude for the role Canada played in the continuation of the Dutch royal line and the family ties of one million Dutch-Canadians with the 'old country' ensure that this bond will remain strong for a long time to come. Princess Margriet, the Dutch princess born in an extra-territorial hospital room in Canada's capital Ottawa symbolizes those ties better than anyone. Upon her most recent visit, she said: "I think Canada is a beautiful country. I think the people are extraordinarily kind and welcoming. It is a country that I really love very much and where I feel at home." Her husband, Pieter van Vollenhoven, quipped as they left Holland Christian Homes in May: "There is a room for us here." And I am sure he can rest assured, should he need it, there would certainly be one ready for him, just like there was a room for his wife-to-be, born in an Ottawa hospital room all those years ago, during the darkest days of Holland's history.

November/December 2017

We're going to Canada

After decades (seven decades to be exact) of denial or willful indifference, there appears to be a sudden, belated upsurge of interest in the post-war migration of half a million Dutch citizens to the traditional 'emigration countries'. It is often the case that interest in a certain aspect of a country's heritage, especially if it is a painful reminder of the past, only surfaces after most of the protagonists are no longer around to tell the story. In the Netherlands it was thus with the history of wartime collaboration. The acceptance of the fact that despite many heroics, there were also a fair number of Dutch people who welcomed and supported the Nazis was long in coming, as was the acknowledgement of the shameful treatment the children of collaborators received after the war. It was thus with coverage of the 'police actions' of the Dutch army in Indonesia, a post-colonial war in which large numbers of young Dutch men were sucked into a conflict that cost many lives and saw many atrocities perpetrated on both sides. And similarly, it appears, it was thus with the migration, forced, or at least strongly encouraged, of large groups of often ill-equipped Dutch citizens.

In the past year, a number of events have taken place that indicate a renewed interest in the emigration wave that lasted from 1947 until around 1964 in which one in twenty Dutch citizens emigrated to various welcoming societies around the globe. It was announced this year that a new emigration museum would be established in Rotterdam, near the place from where most emigrants left the Netherlands. Then earlier this year there was the four-part nationally broadcast television documentary series called *Vaarwel Nederland* (Farewell Netherlands) which focused specifically on the emigrants of the 50s and which devoted an episode each to Canada, the USA, Australia and New Zealand, with a second series covering South Africa, Brazil and Israel. Of the traditional emigration countries, Canada took in by far the most Dutch immigrants. It is fitting then that the third indication of the renewed interest in this period of Dutch history focuses on 'destination Canada' specifically. The *Nederlands Openluchtmuseum* (Dutch Open Air Museum) in Arnhem has refurbished one of its buildings to house a permanent exhibition called *Wij gaan naar Canada* (We're Going to Canada). It was opened in May by Princess Margriet.

The exhibit does a good job of placing the causes of the emigration wave in their historical context. Holland was impoverished after World War II, with the country devastated by five years of occupation, plunder and destruction. There was a severe housing shortage, and large families had to share inadequate housing often with up to four generations in the same space. Many people lodged with relatives or strangers. In her speech from the throne in 1950, Queen Juliana said: "The significant increase in our population and the limitations of available land continue to demand a powerful encouragement of emigration." Essentially, people who ran into issues finding housing, employment or credit were told: "leave the country, you will be better off on the other side of the ocean".

It would be unfair to say that most of those who left were forced against their will. Of course, there are the tragic stories of those who lived the rest of their lives in homesickness and longing for the old country. There are those who would have returned to Holland if only they could have afforded the cost of passage. But there are many who went willingly, sensing opportunities for themselves (and especially for their children) that they did not see in Holland in 1950.

A case in point is the Heersink family of the Achterhoek region of the eastern part of the Netherlands. Jan Heersink was maybe not typical of the first group of emigrants leaving the Netherlands, who were predominantly farmers and farm laborers. Heersink was a mayor. In fact, he was the youngest mayor in the Netherlands when at the age of twenty-seven he became the 'first citizen' of the town of Steenderen. But the emigration fever that spread rapidly through the Netherlands in those years affected him as much as the farm boy up the street. One concern many people in the country had at the time was 'the Russians'. What if the Russians come? It was a common saying in those days, maybe even put more definitively: 'when will the Russians come?'. There was a consensus, so soon after two world wars, that the third was both inevitable and imminent. And no one wanted to suffer through the horrors of another tyrannical occupation. Father Heersink was clear in the matter. He had four sons, two of whom at least would be drafted into Holland's conscription-based army. And they would have to fight the Russians in a cruel war, when push came to shove. So Father Jan, mother Mien and the four boys Ben, Hans, Marnix and Ewout traveled to Canada by plane in 1951. Father Heersink became a fieldman (as they were called at the time) for the *Reformed Church in America*. In effect, that meant that he helped Dutch immigrants of the Hervormd (Reformed) denomination (other denominations had their own fieldmen) get settled in Canada. The fieldmen would help new arrivals find their feet, establish contacts with sponsors, support them in finding a house and also a spiritual home with a fitting congregation.

After some time, Jan Heersink became the vice-consul of the Netherlands in Burlington, Ontario where he had purchased a large house on Lakeshore Road. The house became a welcome home away from home for many new immigrants, who came to the house for advice and help with all manner of administrative matters, but probably even more so, for good old-fashioned Dutch 'gezelligheid'. A glowing Dutch-style stove in the kitchen, hot chocolate, and when the occasion called for it, a glass of Dutch gin (jenever) took the edge off the homesickness for many visitors. The voices and happy laughter may have fallen silent many years ago – Jan Heersink died in 1983, his wife Mien twenty years later – but the house on Lakeshore Road is still there, and it is still used by the sons as offices. If you should ever drive along Lakeshore Road in Burlington, between Guelph Line and Brant Street, keep an eye on the north side of the road. There is a big house with typically Dutch window shutters and the Dutch national coat of arms displayed on the balcony. That's where it all happened.

Jan and Mien Heersink went far beyond what was expected of a vice-consul and spouse. And that community-spirited attitude has rubbed off on the sons. Marnix Heersink is a retired ophthalmologist; he eventually settled in southern Alabama with his American wife Mary. He was the first to contact me about the new Wij gaan naar Canada pavilion at the Open Air Museum and asked me if its grand opening by Princess Margriet would be of interest to DUTCH *the magazine.* Of course it would be! Marnix and his family, as he explained to me, sponsored the pavilion to ensure the story was told and preserved. Without their help, it probably would not be there.

On May 3rd of this year, I made my way to Arnhem early in the morning. By the time the dignitaries were expected for the grand opening of the new pavilion, a crowd had gathered by the entrance to the Midlum Farm, in which the emigration exhibition has been set up. The farm is a typical Friesian Head-Neck-Trunk style farm, which was transferred to the museum, brick by brick, in 1963. As I walked up toward the farm, I encountered a group from Burlington. They were in the country to visit sister-city Apeldoorn to mark Remembrance Day and had gotten wind of the event and wanted to greet 'their' princess, who, after all, is no stranger to the Ontario town with its tight ties with the Netherlands.

Princess Margriet arrived on a historic streetcar, which also carried Mary and Marnix Heersink, Willem Bijleveld, director of the museum, and the mayor of Arnhem. Canada's ambassador to the Netherlands was supposed to be there, but unfortunately she missed the event because she got stuck in traffic on the way to Arnhem from The Hague.

The pavilion makes the history of the emigration wave of the 50s and 60s accessible, clearly explains the reasons behind the mass migration and delves into the experiences of those who left and of those who stayed behind. All captions and descriptions are in both Dutch and English, which makes the exhibition accessible to descendants of the erstwhile emigrants too. Objects and multimedia displays bring the whole experience to life. Special interactive displays include the kitchen table, around which we can hear a Dutch family discuss the pros and cons of emigration and in which we hear the husband try to convince the wife to leave Holland, as was the case in many families. A meeting promoting emigration, of which many were held in the 50s, is re-enacted in a multimedia setting, and one immediately senses the atmosphere of gentle but firm persuasion that typified the whole emigration movement.

Princess Margriet formally opened the meeting by unveiling a 'kist', or a crate, typical of the type that Dutch emigrants used to ship their belongings across the ocean. So iconic are these crates that they feature prominently in both the Pier 21 (Canada's immigration museum) section on the Dutch as in Rosemary Sloot's moving artistic interpretation of her parents' emigration (see page 119).

After the event, I briefly interviewed the princess. She described the exhibition in one word: "Fantastic". She agreed with me that Canada should also have a museum or exhibition devoted to the large influx of Dutch immigrants in the 1950s. Although often invisible, because of their rapid and successful integration, the Dutch did impact Canada thanks to their sheer numbers. When asked what had stood out most in the exhibition for her, the princess said: "how intensely people were induced to leave Holland." And that is something that has long been known to all of us here, living in Canada and the USA, but which long seems to have been forgotten or neglected in the Netherlands. It is encouraging that we are seeing a renewed interest in the subject.

November/December 2018

Immigrant, by Rosemary Sloot

The inescapable burden of the immigrant, forever to be pulled between two worlds' is a quote from Mark Boekelman's introduction to *From the Prairies with Hope* by Jane Aberson. Rosemary Sloot's diptych *Burden of the Immigrant*, bears that motto across the two canvases: on the left a white Canadian landscape, with as its focal point a twig with snow covered dried out thistles, on the right a Dutch country lane, flanked by bare wintry willow trees. The separation is complete: the images stand apart within the shared frame, separating one world, the new Canadian one on the left, from the other, the old Dutch world on the right. There is nothing that seems to bring the two together.

But the two otherwise static landscapes, devoid of life – dried-up flowers, leafless branches – when seen together do have a dynamic element, the spindly twig leaning left, the willows arching right over a ditch, are pulling in opposite directions, ripping the two worlds farther apart than they already are, and with it pulling the onlooker, like the immigrant, between the two.

The starkness of the landscapes reminds us of the emptiness and desolation that virtually every immigrant experiences at one time or another. Old friends and relatives move on, follow the well-trodden country lane around the bend to behind the willow trees, invisible to the onlooker. They have no residual interest in those who left. The immigrant's life in their native country is cut short, their erstwhile course along the road arrested and the future the old world would have held will never be known. In the adopted country everything is new, nothing and no-one is familiar. A field of virgin snow in which tracks still have to be made; the future on the other side of the rift hidden behind a dense forest of towering pine trees. A new land, forbidding, unwelcoming, yet to be discovered.

The image on the right is faint, shimmering with fading memories, the deep-rooted trees of past heritage and family ties take on a dream-like quality, intensified in their reflections in the water-filled ditch – called 'sloot' in Dutch. A coincidence? Or a private reference by the artist to the family name, understood in Holland, but without meaning or history in Canada?

On the other side of the divide, as yet unrooted, in stark contrast to the old willow trees, the fragile thistles, the thin twig ready to be broken by a careless passer-by or a strong gust of wind. But all is not hopeless. With their little snow caps, the dead thistles look like tiny white flowers, a sign of hope, maybe, in a land where one day, after an imprint has been made in the snow and the empty whiteness traversed, the immigrant may reach the not entirely impenetrable forest's edge. And if they endure until the snow melts, the evergreens will take on their natural color. Will their family eventually become as deeply rooted as the old willow trees in that other distant world, as the pines in the new one, or do the fake flowers deceive and are they a false sign of hope? It is the inescapable burden of never knowing what might have been, of the pull between the two worlds.

But is there nowhere the two connect? At first glance the handwritten slogan seems to pull the two pieces together into one story: the story of the immigrant. But even the handwriting is disjointed, just like the two snow covered thistles that seem to grow out of a willow tree across the divide – they do not line up. There is a brief illusion of continuity, but the two worlds will forever pull the immigrant in opposite directions, they do not touch, it is only the immigrant themself who, like the diptych's frame, embraces the two worlds and who knows the full story. A story that starts long before 'the burden' and ends long after 'two worlds', as we see along the bottom of the two disconnected images, where the single sentence, a fragment of a much larger story, both starts and ends outside of our view.

It is this intensely personal, yet universal story that Rosemary's exhibition *Immigrant* tells. When I first saw Rosemary's beautifully detailed paintings, I was stunned by the familiarity of their narrative. And as I saw canvas after canvas a deep sense of melancholy came over me. The images and objects presented in intricate detail come from the Sloot family album and attic. And as I discovered during a long conversation with the artist, they often have an intimately private back story that the casual onlooker will never know. Nevertheless, we recognize them instantly. The divide between old country and new, which is evoked in several of the works – just look at *Final Farewell* with the blurred family portrait behind the young Canadian maple leaves – must resonate with anyone who has made the leap between two countries. Or whose parents or grandparents have.

Rosemary's representation of the story firmly places it in time and space. The dress style, the objects, the letters: Dutch post-war images, the years when half a million people – a full five percent of the nation – stepped onto a boat leaving for Canada, the USA, Australia, New Zealand, South Africa and went, forever, never to see the homeland again, as was the expectation at the time.

Every Dutch family had one of those paraffin burners that we see in *Oliestel* at some point in the post-war era, an essential appliance before the gas was hooked up again – simple reliability after the devastation of World War II. A very useful object to bring along to Canada too, where many families were shocked at the poor state of the accommodation they were given; 'not so much as a nail to hang a tea towel on' as Rosemary's Mother said when they walked into their first house in Canada (a memory recalled in words and images in *Tea Towels*). The words 'origineel' (original) and 'Ned. Fabrikaat' (Made in the Netherlands) on the burner speak volumes.

Anyone with Dutch family roots who remembers the 1950s and 1960s will want to lift the white-veined gray enamel coated pot right off *Arrival*, because their family owned one – had they been standard issue or the only style available during the post-war years of scarcity and rationing? My mother did not get rid of her set until I moved out of the family home. She gave me her pots and pans and finally had an excuse to buy something more modern – the only piece that I did not get, because it had become truly obsolete, was the paraffin burner.

We should be thankful to Rosemary for rescuing a forgotten era, a forgotten tragedy in many cases, from obscurity. She writes in her artist statement: 'Just prior to her death [my strong, pragmatic Mother] quietly told us that she had only one regret and that was immigrating to Canada'. A huge shock to Rosemary, who herself was born in Canada and strongly identifies as Canadian, and a revelation that changed the course of her work. It led her to read the stories of other post-war immigrants to Canada, and it eventually culminated in the collection of 21 works that form Immigrant.

I recognize the story. I have heard it in some form or another dozens of times since in 2008 I took over the publication of *De Krant*. Having only made the jump in 1999, burdening myself forever to be pulled between two worlds – yes, many things may have changed, but that has not – I keep being amazed by the memories not shared with the wider public. Neither Canada, nor the Netherlands seem particularly interested in the almost forgotten story of the time when one in twenty Netherlanders left their native land, almost half of whom arrived in Canada to form, for nearly two decades, the fifth largest ethnic group in the growing nation.

There is a deeply ingrained myth that the Dutch emigrants all fared well in the new land and immediately absorbed the new culture and never looked back – and to be fair, this holds true for many of them. But a friend of mine whose mother lost half of her large family to emigration – not something that I knew until weeks before I left myself, the big emigration wave of the 40s and 50s is rarely mentioned in Holland – told me to my great and rather naïve surprise as he thought about a particular uncle: "you should not believe that they were all happy and successful in Canada."

And with that, the story which sometimes seems to have taken on a mythical aspect is brought right back to the real world again. A real world in which the Dutch are no different from the many other immigrant groups that came to Canada and the USA over the centuries. And therefore, this exhibition should appeal to anyone who wants to understand the eternal pull the immigrant experiences between old and new, between there and here, regardless of ethnicity. However meager the belongings brought across, they are the last tangible treasured remnants of a lost world, a lost life. A photograph, a tea tin, something as mundane as a ladle can become a treasured symbol of a world distant, dear, but forever lost.

In her highly accomplished, at times almost photographically realistic, style Rosemary's painting brings the emotions of the immigrant and their burden across in its most raw and tactile form. Her work should be looked at it with an eye for detail and for symbolism. Each one, like Burden of the Immigrant, carries a huge amount of meaning, of story, for every one of us, although our stories may differ in the details. For this exhibition Rosemary has created a collection of works that should be recognized as a significant addition to the representation of a quintessential Canadian experience – are we not all immigrants? – in modern art.

May/June 2012

The paintings in the exhibition have been collected in the book 'Immigrant, From the Postwar Netherlands to Canada in 21 Paintings'. The book contains extensive notes on the paintings by the artist and other background material. It is available on Mokeham Publishing's dutchthestore.com website.

Sixty Years of Dutch Groceries in Greater Vancouver

One of the most enduring legacies of the large post-war migration of people from the Netherlands to Canada are the Dutch stores. Scattered around the countryside in Ontario and British Columbia, they often form the last visible proof of a once thriving Dutch-Canadian community. Although the total number of stores has dwindled, they seem to live on surprisingly long in comparison to other Dutch-Canadian institutions such as social clubs, travel agencies, soccer clubs and cultural organizations. Food is such a comforter and is so entwined with our identity, taking us back to our earliest childhood, that its particular appeal lasts much longer than the desire to get together with compatriots or travel to the ancestral land.

One day almost twenty years ago, a few months after I had arrived in Canada, living in a town without a Dutch store (I had not even yet discovered that they existed), I was driving along the mountainous roads of British Columbia on a work assignment when I came to the small town of Keremeos in the Similkameen Valley. Along the side of the road, I saw a fruit stand with a sign that read 'Fresh Fruit and Dutch Imports'. I stopped and got out of the car. A half-open shed was adorned with faded KLM-posters showing tulip fields and windmills. In crates and on shelves next to the apples, peaches and plums from the owner's orchard were packs of speculaas cookies, ontbijtkoek (Dutch gingerbread), cans of kale and jars of appelmoes (apple sauce). To the right was the archetypal self-service section for bulk licorice, and behind the counter was a cooler with cheese and smoked fish. Also behind the counter stood an old lady who told me she was well into her eighties. Yes, she said in fluent Dutch with a hint of a Rotterdam accent, she did brisk business in the summer months when tourists came to visit the area. Besides, there was a sizeable Dutch community in the small town. And her son-in-law made deliveries around the area. I bought some goodies including one of her homemade boterkoeks (Dutch shortbread), which to this day I still remember as the best boterkoek I ever ate. When I got home, I was a hero.

Unfortunately, I soon discovered that the fruit stand closed shop completely in winter and was at best an unreliable source of Dutch imports. By necessity, their assortment was limited. That is when we discovered *Holland Shopping Centre (HSC)* in New Westminster. Although depending on the state of the mountain passes it was a four to five-hour drive from our home in Penticton, it became our regular supplier of Dutch food items. Now, I have to clarify that it is not as if we got our daily groceries from HSC (although with the exception of fresh produce we could have), but on occasion, and especially on special occasions such as Easter, Sinterklaas or Christmas, a Dutch family wants Dutch stuff. Fortunately, HSC ships, and many a box of goodies made its way across the Coastal Mountain Range to the Okanagan Valley. Actually, as I discovered later, HSC does a brisk business shipping groceries across North America, including into the USA. They even receive overseas orders and have shipped as far afield as Japan and Australia.

Over the years we got to know the owners of HSC (Tako and Frances Slump) well, especially after I started publishing *De Krant* and HSC became one of our most loyal advertisers. This year HSC celebrates sixty years in business. A good occasion, I thought, to delve a little into its history and current success. I met with Tako in the 'gezellig' coffee corner of the Chilliwack location of Holland Shopping Centre, and as I enjoyed a 'frikandel speciaal' (a fried sausage topped with sauces and onions and made right behind the store in a state-of-the art production facility), we talked about the history and legacy of the store.

The store started long before Tako had even moved to Canada. In 1952, a former coalman from The Hague called John de

Haas started peddling excess produce from his vegetable garden among his fellow Dutch immigrants in the New Westminster area. One day, one of his clients asked him if he knew where he could get a Dutch smoked sausage (rookworst) to go with the kale he had just purchased. De Haas knew just the place, and thus he branched out and started delivering imported and locally produced Dutch goods along with his own crops.

After a successful run of a few years, the authorities suggested that to ensure he complied with bylaws and ordinances, he should settle down and start selling his wares from a fixed location rather than the back of his truck. And thus in 1958, John de Haas and his wife Helen opened Holland Shopping Centre on Kingsway, on the boundary of New Westminster and Burnaby, near the banks of the mighty Fraser River in coastal British Columbia.

The successful business moved several times, and in 1981 John's son Bas with his wife Alice took over the store. Among other improvements, the new owners launched a catalog business and started shipping their Dutch products to clients outside of the Greater Vancouver Area, bringing home comforts to Dutch immigrants who lived remotely or in towns without a dedicated Dutch store.

In the meantime, Tako and Frances were growing up in Slochteren in the province of Groningen. They knew each other from a young age, "same street, same school, same church," Tako told me, and were destined for each other. Another thing that seemed to be clear from an early age was that Tako would leave the Netherlands. Tako's grandfather Rinke Slump Sr. was the leader of a group of pioneers consisting of members of the *Reformed Churches in the Netherlands (Liberated)* who started an agricultural colony in Brazil near Monte Alegre. In tow was Rinke's family, including Tako's father Heiko, who returned to the Netherlands in 1963. Heiko always told Tako 'Holland is too small'. In 1992, a first exploratory trip to North America took place, and the decision was made: it was going to be somewhere in North America.

When in 1995 the opportunity arose to purchase HSC, Frances and Tako jumped at it. Together with Frances's sister and her husband Bram Eigenraam, the couple moved to British Columbia. Did he have any experience in retail, I asked Tako. "No, I was a millwright by trade. I knew nothing about being a retailer. Neither did Frances. But I like to fix things and make them the way I like. And I like a challenge." And thus a new phase began in the history of HSC.

This phase was based on renewal coupled with tradition. While the physical store remains the anchor of the business, in 2000 the first website with an e-commerce component was launched. While the catalog was mailed once a year to a set group of customers, the online store opened HSC to the world and allowed for real-time updates of products and stock. By 2011, the catalog had become obsolete, and now hollandshop.com is the go-to destination.

In 2002, a second location was opened in Chilliwack, which has a large Dutch heritage population. The store on Young Road, one of Chilliwack's thoroughfares, quickly became a favored destination for the Dutch-Canadians of the Upper Fraser Valley.

Famous Dutch soccer player and philosopher Johan Cruyff once said "every disadvantage has its advantage," or to use the more common albeit slightly hackneyed phrase: every problem is an opportunity. All it needs is the insight, will and initiative to see the opportunity and turn the disadvantage into an advantage. When in 2007 HSC's regular supplier of Dutch deli meats and croquettes decided to close his business, something needed to be done, because a Dutch store without those products is not a true Dutch store. So Tako decided to recruit an old friend from the Netherlands, a master butcher, and the *Meester Jan* brand of croquettes, frikandels and other Dutch delicacies was born. The production facility behind the store in Chilliwack produces some of the best snack meats in North America.

I wonder what the most popular items in the store are. Without hesitation, Tako answers: "Cheese and candy, especially licorice (drop)." Canada's strict protectionist import quotas on dairy sometimes make life difficult for cheese lovers, but Tako has some good news: since last year, HSC has acquired a cheese quota, which means that it can import a certain amount of cheese with lower duties. This has allowed him to bring in different types of specialty cheese that he could not stock in the past. But you can't run a Dutch store with just cheese and drop. HSC stocks more than 2500 items, some of which may sell less than ten a year. "You have to give people what they want," says Tako. "I have to have a wide selection. I want to be a full-service Dutch store." And if by chance that one particular item from the Netherlands that a customer really craves is not available, HSC will do a special order and bring it in from the Netherlands. That's how you make people happy.

Another way to make people happy is to support community activities. Frances and Tako have always volunteered at community events such as Sinterklaas and King's Day, and HSC can often be found among the list of event sponsors. The profits from the booth they run at the annual Sinterklaas event go back to the organizing committee. Local Dutch society *Je Maintiendrai* has a free lending library that has shelf space in the New Westminster store.

HSC is the largest Dutch store in Western Canada, and in terms of sheer selection, I would not be surprised if it was the best stocked in all of North America. The enduring legacy of Dutch stores is summed up nicely by the craving that even the third generation Dutch still have for the food that Oma made. A Dutch store owner in Toronto once told me that as the number of original immigrants dwindles, their grandchildren are better customers than their children. It was Opa and Oma who brought the grandkids to the store and raised them on good Dutch home-style foods as they took care of them when their moms and dads were at work. And it seems that the love of good food is passed down to younger generations. Talking to Tako about his client base, the Chilliwack store is still very much rooted in the original immigrant community and its descendants. The New Westminster store, conveniently located in the Greater Vancouver Area, draws more expats and newer immigrants. And non-Dutch clients who have done a stint in the Netherlands and have grown to appreciate Dutch products have also found their way to the store.

The fruit stand in Keremeos stopped selling Dutch stuff a few years ago, but fortunately for the inhabitants of the Similkameen and Okanagan Valley and far beyond, HSC can be relied upon to ship its Dutch products wherever its clients need them. Although nothing beats browsing in the HSC stores in New Westminster and Chilliwack, where apart from cheese, candy and ontbijt-koek, you can choose from 2500 other products, including issues of *DUTCH, the magazine.*

July/August 2018

The Friesian Horse Association of North America

Friesian horses are majestic. They are graceful, compact, strong and have a long, full and wavy mane and tail. They are usually black, and except for occasionally a small star on their heads, they have no other markings. Sometimes, one will encounter a very dark brown specimen. Friesians have a fine head with short, pointed ears. The breed is known for its lively, high-stepped gait. Friesians are considered to be active and energetic, yet soft and agreeable. Altogether they are very elegant horses.

Friesian horses also have a long, proud history – like Friesland, the country they hail from. Early descriptions of the breed date back to Roman times, when it was used by Friesian cavalry units. Depictions of knights riding with William the Conqueror in the 11th century show horses that have a remarkable resemblance to modern-day Friesians. Although there was probably some interbreeding with Arabic and Andalusian horses during the crusades and the Eighty Years' War, there appears to be a long lineage of Friesian horses dating back to the early historic period. In 1544, a Friesian horse is first mentioned in an actual document when it was recorded that John Frederick I, Elector of Saxony, traveled to the *Reichstag* in Speyer on a Friesian stallion.

By the late 18th and early 19th century, the breed was increasingly only to be found in Friesland. Because a Friesian is not an ideal workhorse, owning one became a measure of wealth, a status symbol for rich gentleman farmers. It was generally used to go to church on Sundays, and although the Friesian is not a racehorse, farmers would race each other over short distances in local events.

Because the Friesian was not particularly suited to farm work, by the middle of the 19th century, many farmers had switched to sturdier animals. Friesians were often interbred with other breeds. Yet a small and dedicated group of horse lovers wanted to preserve the unique characteristics of the Friesian breed, and in 1879, the Friesian studbook was founded in Reduzum, Friesland by three dedicated breeders. It was the first studbook in the Netherlands, which to this day is maintained by the *Vereniging Koninklijk Fries Paarden-Stamboek (KFPS)* (Royal Friesian Horses Studbook Association).

Despite the specialized attention which came with the studbook, the mechanization of farming and the overall transition from a more rural to a more urban lifestyle almost brought the Friesian horse to extinction. By the mid-1960s, there were only five hundred mares and just three approved breeding stallions registered in the studbook.

A group of enthusiasts decided that the beautiful Friesian breed should be preserved. An intense campaign of resuscitation began in 1967 with a promotional tour through southwestern Friesland, when a group of the remaining Friesians was ridden from Huis ter Heide near St. Nicolaasga to Workum. Several riding clubs joined the campaign as people started to rediscover the versatility and beauty of the breed. The campaign was ultimately wildly successful. From fewer than one thousand individuals in 1967, the population of registered Friesian horses has grown to more than seventy thousand worldwide today. And worldwide is not an exaggeration. As Friesian emigrants took an interest in the horse of their homeland, and as horse lovers everywhere started to appreciate the special characteristics of the breed, breeders in many countries started to specialize in Friesians. Currently, there are Friesians registered in more than seventy countries.

To be registered, Friesians have to undergo stringent inspections (called 'keuringen' in Dutch). Horses are first inspected as foals and then again when they have passed the age of three. They have to pass the inspection to be entered into the studbook. The horses are classified according to their characteristics, and about twenty-five percent of mares are given a 'star' designation, the highest accolade available. Stallions have to get a special 'breeding designation', and only horses descended from these approved studbook stallions may be entered into the registry of Friesian horses. So rigorous is this inspection, that there are only about one hundred approved breeding stallions among the seventy thousand or so Friesian horses. Because the inspections are so stringent and the original stock was so small, and because relatively few stallions are approved, there is a risk of excessive inbreeding, which is a common issue with purebreds in any species. The association actively ensures that congenital disorders are identified and that the afflicted horses are not allowed to breed, which ensures a healthy population and avoids the potentially negative effects of maintaining a purebred stock of animals.

The first organized studbook outside of the Netherlands was initiated by a group of breeders in North America who held an exploratory meeting in Visalia, California in 1983 to discuss the formation of a North American association. The *Friesian Horse Association of North America (FHANA)* was formally instituted in 1984 and became the guardian of the first non-Dutch certified studbook, under the auspices and direction of the KFPS. From a small start with several dedicated breeders, mostly immigrants from Friesland, the association has grown to boast more than eight thousand horses in its studbook. There are sixteen chapters, spread across the continent, from Southern California to Quebec and the Canadian Maritime provinces, and including states with strong equestrian traditions such as Kentucky and Texas. Areas with large Dutch and particularly Friesian immigrant populations are, of course, well-represented, and there are breeders and associations in California, Michigan, Ontario and British Columbia. In Ontario, a show event is organized near Tillsonburg, on or around Labor Day every year.

One of the most active chapters of FHANA is the *Alberta Friesian Horse Association (AFHA)*. It was founded in the mid-1990s and needed a minimum of six breeders to have the Friesian horse formally recognized by the *Alberta Agriculture Equine Department*. In 1997, AFHA successfully achieved registration as an official breed in the province.

AFHA was awarded the 'chapter of the year' award by FHANA five years in a row, and it is therefore fitting that AFHA was given the honor of hosting the official thirty-five-year anniversary celebration of FHANA. The event, with activities spread out over three days, from July 15th to 17th, 2019, took place in Ponoka, Alberta. After having been approached by one the organizers, Annie Muilwijk, a breeder from Bentley near Lacombe in Alberta, I decided to attend the event. As a bonus, I managed to persuade Friesian author Hylke Speerstra, whose books we publish in English translation (see page 101), to join the group of fifty enthusiasts who traveled from the Netherlands to attend the event. One of the chapters in his iconic book about Dutch emigration, *Cruel Paradise*, tells the fascinating story of Klaas and Mares van der Ploeg, breeders of Friesian horses in Ithaca, Michigan. Hylke was on-hand to sign his books after taking in the Calgary Stampede – valuable research for his next book, he told me.

Ponoka is in the heart of Alberta horse country – the *Calnash Ag Event Centre* where the FHANA celebration took place is home to the *Ponoka Stampede*, second only to the *Calgary Stampede* in Canada – and coincidentally also in the heart of Alberta Dutch country. From the early 1990s until the early 2000s, large numbers of Dutch farmers moved away from the Netherlands because of milk quota and other pressures on their livelihood. Many of them settled in Alberta.

On the evening of the 15th, we were treated to a campfire welcome, with locally produced Dutch snack food such as frikandels, croquettes and of course, fries with mayonnaise and spicy peanut sauce.

The second day was the main program day. By 10 a.m. more than five hundred people had gathered in the event center, and more than one thousand would attend over the course of the day. The bleachers were full, and the Canadian, American and Dutch national anthems were played. After that, there was a brief, awkward silence. Something was missing … A lone voice in the audience started to sing: 'Frysk bloed tsjoch op! Wol no ris brûze en siede …' and soon at least half of the assembled audience joined in and a spontaneous rendering of *De Alde Friezen* (The Old Friesians), the Friesian anthem, reverberated through the arena. A thunderous applause followed, and a day full of equestrian showmanship and mastery started.

In total, I counted forty-two events – I may be off by one or two – in which more than sixty different horses participated. The events varied from spectacularly timed races around obstacles with so-called marathon carts, to pure dressage displays to classical music, and from themed displays such as a western ride, rides in historic period dress and a Star Wars themed ride, to acrobatic horseback performances worthy of the circus, which happens to be an environment in which Friesians have long been popular.

Of special interest was the Ringsteken (Ring sticking) competition. Ringsteken is a traditional Dutch event in which a horse rider or a passenger in a horse-drawn carriage attempts to stick an object like a stick or a lance through a ring mounted on a pole while riding past. Points are awarded for a successful attempt. Ringsteken is a popular pastime at fairs and markets in various regions of the Netherlands. In the Friesian variant, the person doing the sticking is the passenger in a traditional horse-drawn carriage called a sjees. A sjees is a light carriage, with two large, round fourteen-spoke wheels. The word is derived from the French chaise (chair).

Sjeeses were also used in the spectacular grand finale to the event, a Friesian quadrille, aptly rechristened Alberta quadrille for the occasion. In a Friesian quadrille, eight sjeeses perform a carefully choreographed display of riding skill that is breathtaking to watch if performed well. And this quadrille was performed well, partially thanks to the dedication of the riders who had rehearsed every two weeks for a full year to attain the perfection on display in Ponoka. On the third day, the participants were treated to a bus tour along several Alberta Friesian breeding stables. The three-day event was a triumph of Friesian equestrian fellowship and a fitting celebration of thirty-five years of FHANA.

Because of its majestic looks and its easygoing temperament, the Friesian horse is a favorite in movies. Zorro is usually given a Friesian, although historically that is, of course, an anomaly. Other recent films or TV shows in which Friesians have performed include *Conan the Barbarian, Eragon, Alexander, The Chronicles of Narnia, Clash of the Titans* and *The Hunger Games.* One of the first movies in which a Friesian (named Othello) played a major role was *Ladyhawke* (1985), starring Michelle Pfeiffer and Dutch actor Rutger Hauer. Hauer was an avid rider and had already worked with Friesians on the set of TV series *Floris* in the Netherlands. Throughout the time when he lived in North America, he owned a Friesian horse and was a long-time member of the KFPS. Hauer died two days after the FHANA event in Alberta ended, on July 19th, 2019 (see page 190). At his funeral, his casket was carried on a traditional wagon drawn by two Friesian horses.

Thirty-five years after FHANA was formally founded, the Friesian horse has become a popular breed in North America and throughout the world. There is no doubt that the breed's popularity will continue to rise. Many owners of Friesian horses, through their active participation in keurings and events, will have learned that their beloved ride hails originally from a small corner of northwestern Europe, from a land called Friesland. A land where they are proud of their independence, individualism, sportsmanship, and beautiful language. A land where they are proud of their horses. And rightfully so.

November/December 2019

The Judge, by Jesse van Muylwijck

When I took over the editorship of *De Krant* in 2008, my wife Petra immediately told me that I should spruce the old publication up a bit with a comic strip. A very good piece of advice, with which I wholeheartedly agreed. There was just one problem: Where do you find a comic strip that fits the editorial focus of a Dutch-language monthly newspaper for immigrants to Canada and the USA, preferably one that is also topical and entertaining? As the first few issues appeared, Petra kept reminding me, and I kept racking my brain about where to find a suitable comic.

Two years later, March 2010, and Petra had given up reminding me. We were visiting Vancouver, where the Winter Olympics were taking place. The Dutch Prime Minister of the time, Jan-Peter Balkenende, was in town to visit the games, and he held a reception for the Dutch community. At the reception, I was talking to two-time *Eleven Cities Tour* winner Evert van Benthem and his wife, who live in Alberta, when Petra suddenly pulled me by my shoulder and said excitedly: "There's someone you must meet." I tried to shrug her off, pointing to the legendary skater, but she insisted. So I politely took my leave from the Van Benthems, and Petra pulled me over to a friendly young gentleman with wire-rimmed glasses. "This is Jesse," she said. "He draws a comic strip."

"Jesse van Muylwijck," he introduced himself. "I make *De Rechter* (The Judge)," he said. "De Rechter, I know that strip. I always used to read it in the *Leeuwarder Courant* when we lived in Leeuwarden."

"That's possible," said Jesse. "The strip appears in a large number of Dutch regional newspapers."

I wondered why Jesse was at a Dutch consular event on the Canadian West Coast if he published a topical daily comic strip about Dutch current affairs in the Netherlands. "I live on Vancouver Island," he explained. "With the Internet these days, that is very possible. I can stay up to date about Dutch politics and society through the Internet, and I email my strip to the newspapers."

I was amazed, and also a little starstruck. I am a great fan of comic strips and had always enjoyed De Rechter.

I explained to Jesse that in a sense I also published a regional Dutch newspaper, even if the region was North America and not Twente or South Limburg. I asked if I could publish De Rechter in De Krant. Everything was arranged while we enjoyed a Heineken and some bitterballen, courtesy of the Consulate General of the Kingdom of the Netherlands in Vancouver.

When a year later I made plans to launch an English-language magazine about the Netherlands, I got in touch with Jesse. He agreed to supply an English translation of the strip I selected from the approximately sixty that he drew in each two-month period. That gave me a good selection. I always try to select a strip that does not require intimate knowledge of Dutch current affairs, but that does display an innate 'Dutchness', whether in the subject matter, or simply in the drawing. And since that first issue of *DUTCH the magazine* in the fall of 2011, we have published a strip by Jesse in each edition.

Last year De Rechter celebrated its twenty-fifth anniversary, and June this year, will mark the launch of the first appearance of the Dutch judge in an English-language book. Every year Jesse collects the best two hundred of the three hundred strips created in the past year in a book. But thus far, these have only been regularly published in Dutch (although there has also been an Italian translation). Coming June *The Judge: A Touch of Dutch* will appear in the Netherlands, in English. Two good reasons to find out a little more about the Dutch comic artist who lives on the far west coast of Canada and has managed to write and draw a topical Dutch comic strip six days a week, for twenty-six years.

In the early 1990s, newspaper strip pages in the Netherlands generally had translations of American syndicated comic strips like *Peanuts, Hagar the Horrible* and the *Wizard of Id*. Original Dutch newspapers' strips were often rooted in a different style developed in the 1930s, with a strip of drawings, but instead of (or in addition to) text bubbles, the narrative would be written out under the image, in full paragraphs of text. Examples of these are classics like *Kapitein Rob* and the much beloved *Tom Poes* strips written by Dutch strip icon Marten Toonder.

That is not to say that the Netherlands does not have a strip culture. On the contrary, homegrown comic strips are wildly popular, rooted in the European – mainly Belgian/French – tradition, but with a strong Dutch flavor. They are mostly disseminated either in dedicated strip magazines, or in comic albums. These albums generally contain a complete narrative story (like *Tintin, Asterix, Lucky Luke, Suske & Wiske*), or consist of collected 'gag' strips. The latter include *Gaston* (Guust in Dutch translation), written by Franco-Belgian master and one of Jesse's great influences André Franquin (1924-1997), and *Jan, Jans en de Kinderen* (Jan, Jans and the Children), written by Dutchman Jan Kruis (1933-2017). These strips differ from American strips in that they generally cover two or four bands and fit on a half or full magazine page. Conversely, the *Marvel* genre of comics with superheroes like *Batman* and *Superwoman* only exists in translation in the Netherlands. There is no comparable homegrown tradition.

When Jesse first decided to try selling his new single-band strip to newspapers in the Netherlands, one of his selling points was: 'American strips often lose something in their translation to Dutch, but an original Dutch strip is very recognizable for Dutch readers.' And after pitching his strip to a syndicate of Dutch regional newspapers and to a number of individual publications, the first Rechter strip appeared on August 30th, 1993 in the *Rotterdams Dagblad* (Rotterdam Daily News). A week later, Jesse received the great news that the syndicate was interested too, and that twelve newspapers would start publishing the strip. That was the official beginning, but to get to that point, Jesse had been preparing for three years, developing the characters and drawing 144 sample instalments. Preparations had really started many years earlier, as Jesse had always been an avid artist who had started drawing at the age of four, had his first comic strips published when he was twelve and started to get paid for them at the age of fifteen.

Nevertheless, he decided he should also be prepared to have a 'real' career. So he went to law school, graduating from *Groningen University* in 1985. But when a legal firm offered him a job, he knew that drawing had at least as big a pull on him as the law, and he continued his post-secondary education at Groningen Art School *Minerva*.

When around 1990 he started toying with the idea of drawing a daily syndicated newspaper strip, his two passions came together in a perfect symbiosis, and *The Judge* was born.

With his intimate knowledge of how things work in the courtroom, Jesse started The Judge with a limited set of characters and predominantly courtroom-based stories. The original four characters are the judge, a lawyer, a court clerk and a court security officer. This limited the universe of discourse to the courtroom and criminal law. After some time, the subject matter expanded, first into civil law and later into the judge's private life. A large number of additional characters appeared, including a second lawyer, a court reporter and her little daughter, a prosecutor, a bailiff, a notary, a law clerk and last but not least, in strip number 484, the judge's wife.

The judge is an affable older gentleman who is slightly out of touch with the modern world, but with a keen mind, a fondness for justice and fair play, and an undeniable sense of sharp and sometimes absurdist humor. Jesse has surrounded him with contrasting characters like a wife who thrives on activity, while the judge would rather sit quietly in a corner and work, or the worldly cut-throat, money-grabbing lawyer. This creates a natural tension, which according to Jesse is ideal in storytelling, offering myriad opportunities for a small story or gag to develop. Jesse makes it sound easier than I'm sure it really is, and I have a deep admiration for his ability to come up with a new three-frame funny story six days a week, fifty-two weeks a year against a strict deadline. Jesse is well prepared and takes notes and makes little sketches of things he encounters throughout the day. To ensure that he'll never be stuck, he has a binder full of these ideas, half-finished strips and notes. But fortunately, he always seems to have inspiration and does not need his backup plan.

In 2005, Jesse, his wife and business partner Marleen, daughter Yip and son Bo moved to Vancouver Island. Why? Because it is a beautiful place, far away from hectic Holland, where you can work in peace, Jesse told me.

When they first moved, Marleen and Jesse were concerned that their Dutch clients, the newspaper editors, could be suspicious of his ability to keep creating a 'Dutch' strip, if he lived an ocean and a continent away. So the Van Muylwijck family moved to British Columbia without telling their clients, viewing it as a purely private matter. They set up a local phone line in the Netherlands with voice mail and if the quality of the work was not affected, why would it be an issue? And the best way to prove that, was to just do it and make sure that no one would notice anything different in the strips being submitted every day. It worked! One of the newspaper editors accidentally found out six months after the immigration to Canada. He mentioned it at a syndicate editors' meeting, and the majority view was one of amused admiration. Quite the stunt, was the general consensus at the meeting, especially since no one had detected any change in the strip. The Internet and regular trips to Holland keep Jesse informed. And for fourteen years now, one of Holland's most popular newspaper comics has been created in Canada!

In addition to his daily strip, Jesse also performs as a 'stand-up cartoonist', a term he himself coined. As a stand-up cartoonist, he applies his observation skills and drawing talent at company meetings and conferences. With a quickly drawn cartoon, he can often cut directly to the core of a debate. Cartoons can be used to open sensitive subjects up for discussion. They can provoke and challenge, thereby increasing the involvement of the participants. Jesse has worked as a stand-up cartoonist for multinational companies such as Heineken, Philips and Rabobank and continues to appear at events across Europe and North America.

In 2010, Jesse was awarded the prestigious *Stripschapprijs* (Comic Strip Guild Prize), the only comic strip award in the Netherlands. De Rechter was the subject of special exhibitions in the *Nederlands Stripmuseum* (Dutch National Comic Strip Museum) in Groningen in 2011 and again in 2018 to celebrate the twenty-fifth anniversary of the strip.

So since 2005, The Judge is created in Canada, but appreciated and read predominantly in the Netherlands. Since 1993, Jesse has created almost eight thousand instalments of De Rechter. The cartoons have been collected in more than thirty Dutch language books for which Marleen does the production, graphic design and sales. It is therefore fitting that one of Holland's most beloved cartoon characters will now also be available in a book in English. Now Jesse's neighbors on Vancouver Island and comic lovers throughout the English-speaking world can get to know Jesse's judge and the cast of characters supporting him.

With his crisp drawing style and dry sense of humor, Jesse van Muylwijck has created a comic strip that belongs in the top echelons of the genre of the single-band, three-to-four-frame comic. The jokes span the gamut from courtroom-inspired humor, to mild political satire, to puns and wordplay, to philosophical aphorism. Some of them may be difficult to translate and transpose to a different culture, but in the vast majority of them, the humor and humanity of the strip shine through the translation.

May/June 2019

Bronte Village

As long-time readers of *DUTCH the magazine* know, the *Place* section has been a recurring feature since our very first issue. And unlike some other features which we have occasionally skipped for lack of space or for our themed commemorative Liberation issues in 2015 and 2020, we never missed Place. The places we visited in those commemorative issues fit with the overall theme of remembrance, when we looked at the National WWII monuments on Amsterdam's Dam Square and at Waalsdorpervlakte respectively.

As we were brainstorming the contents for our tenth anniversary issue that would appear in September, 2021, we discussed what 'place' would be a fitting location to include in this issue. Is there a place that best typifies ten years of *DUTCH the magazine*? And ultimately we decided it might be fitting to highlight the place where *DUTCH the magazine* is produced. Our own office, in Oakville, Ontario, and to give you a little peek behind the scenes.

Now before we do that it should be emphasized that *DUTCH* does not get created entirely in our Oakville office. To begin with there are the freelance contributors, many of whom have been with us since the early days, who work from their own homes or offices and submit their work electronically. We also do not print the magazine at our Oakville office. The magazine is printed in Burnaby, British Columbia, and then mailed out from Vancouver for our Canadian subscribers and Blaine, Washington, for our American subscribers. But our Oakville office is the hub of our creative and administrative process. It is where the magazine originates.

The Oakville office is not our first office. *Mokeham Publishing*, which publishes the magazine, was founded in 2007, and we started out in a small shed in my backyard in the Redlands neighborhood of Penticton, British Columbia. Initially, that was just for the production of *De Krant*. But it was in that ninety-square-foot shed that the first work towards starting an English language publication, that would eventually become *DUTCH the magazine*, took place.

As I was working on plans to launch the magazine, we also published our first books in *The Dutch in Wartime* series. With the added administrative work and need for more space and storage, we moved the operation to our own dedicated office at 457 Ellis Street in downtown Penticton.

And it was in this office in Penticton that our first issue (September/October 2011) was put together. I still vividly remember brainstorming the masthead layout design and cover of that first issue. I had mocked up proofs in four different styles and showed these to anyone who was prepared to give an opinion.

A special occasion was when the Consul-General of the Netherlands in Vancouver came over to Penticton for the official opening of our office. He was joined by Penticton Mayor Dan Ashton and Member of Parliament Dan Albas.

Then in 2013 the big move east happened. We emptied out our office, and everything was loaded onto a truck for the 2,500-mile drive to our new location at 2465 Lakeshore Road West in the town of Oakville. Oakville is part of the Greater Toronto Area (GTA) and is smack in the center of the Golden Horseshoe, Ontario's economic hub. Ontario also happens to be the province where half of Canada's one million people of Dutch descent live, which makes it an ideal base for attending Dutch cultural events, which are more numerous and more widely attended here than anywhere else in North America.

Our office is about five miles outside the downtown core of Oakville, in an area of town called Bronte. Bronte is a former fishing village on the shores of Lake Ontario – our office is a block from the lake. As we moved to Bronte, I discovered that the village itself has a bit of a Dutch connection. A number of Dutch families settled here in the 1950s to farm or run small businesses, several of which are still owned and run by children or grandchildren of the original immigrants. I have not been able to verify this, but according to some of my local sources, Bronte at one time had a branch of a Dutch-Canadian credit union and a Dutch store. Not much is visibly left of the Dutch presence in Bronte, except our office on the corner of Lakeshore Road and Bronte Road, a busy intersection and a plaque on the facade of the Bronte Canadian Legion Hall, which reads:

1945 – 1970
IN APPRECIATION
This plaque is presented to the Canadian Legions of Oakville Ontario
By the Dutch-Canadian Entertainment Club
In Commemoration of the 25th Anniversary of the Liberation of the Netherlands, 1945.

We are also less than a mile removed from the border between Oakville and the city of Burlington. Burlington has strong Dutch connections. It is twinned with the city of Apeldoorn, celebrates *Canada Netherlands Friendship Day* with a ceremony at city hall every year on May 5th and boasts a Dutch store, a Dutch retirement home and a branch of Dutch-Canadian Credit Union *DUCA*, all within a few miles of our office.

Although our office is not really meant to be a retail space, its shop front does allow for walk-ins. And before the pandemic we would occasionally get local subscribers come in to hand-deliver their renewal checks or pick up a magazine or book. We always welcomed this, as it created a direct connection with our readers, although only few of our subscribers live close enough to do this.

Some of the best encounters have been with the unsuspecting. The people who came to Bronte for other reasons – it is a bustling area with lots of restaurants, a marina, a beach and a lakeside park – who saw the signs above our storefront and were curious about what we are.

Note, however, that we are definitely not set up as a retail space. We only have two desks in the one-room space, from which all the work is done. We also have a small library of books about the Netherlands and the Dutch diaspora, and of course, back copies of magazines, newspapers and copies of the books we publish. However, the most convenient way to connect with us is still through email, phone and our website contact form, but having said that, we are very happy with our little bit of physical Dutchness in the GTA.

September/October 2021

REFLECTION

Wartime Hero Who Had Room in Her House for Everyone
Tina Strobos (1920-2012)

When at the age of 85 Dr. Tina Strobos lobbied her fellow residents at her seniors' home in Westchester County, New York, to take in victims of Hurricane Katrina, she was following a time-honored family tradition. More than 90 years earlier, during World War I, her grandmother had taken in displaced Belgian and Austrian war refugees. During World War II, in Nazi-occupied Holland, Dr. Strobos and her mother opened their doors again, at severe risk to themselves. When in a 1985 interview she talked about this episode in her life, she said: "We never questioned the premise, as if this was a tradition in the family. Well, it was. For us it was the right thing to do."

At the start of the war Dr. Strobos – then 19-year old medical student Tineke Buchter – and her mother Marie Schotte lived in an old three story house in central Amsterdam, not far from where some years later Anne Frank and her family would hide. Within five days of the German invasion the two of them took in their first fugitive from the Nazi occupying forces, Henri Polak, a pioneering Dutch labor leader, who, as a prominent, politically active, Jew was at high risk of immediate incarceration. More than one hundred people, Jews, members of the resistance, and political 'undesirables' would follow as the two women continued to operate a transit house for the Dutch resistance during the full five years of the German occupation.

A carpenter working for the resistance installed a hiding place in the attic. On the second floor an alarm was installed to warn those hiding there of Gestapo raids. They could escape out of a top floor window onto the roof of an adjacent school. Being instinctively cautious, Dr. Strobos never understood why Anne Frank's family did not plan an escape route.

Dr. Strobos carefully forged id-cards – which she pickpocketed at various events – for Jews to pass as non-Jewish. She transported Jewish people, many of them children separated from their parents to their hiding places in the countryside. She smuggled supplies, ration cards, radios, and forged documents through roadblocks. She also brought her lonely and isolated charges a much-needed friendly word, some human comfort in an often alien, disorientating and always dangerous environment. And despite regular raids on their home by the Gestapo – who seized and interrogated her nine times – Dr. Strobos and her mother kept taking in people. If discovered, any one of their activities would be enough to expose them to extreme torture and eventually execution.

Dr. Strobos's son Jur explained to me that to do what his mother did, and do it successfully, four qualities, which she possessed in ample measure, were required: a strong moral compass impervious to external pressures, a solid social network, innate charisma with leadership abilities, and an empathetic nature. Her moral compass was not rooted in religion, but rather in the idealism of the early 20th century socialist movement. Tina Strobos was a proud, self-proclaimed 'third-generation atheist', something which sent at least one *Welcome Wagon* lady who visited when Dr. Strobos settled in South Carolina in the early 1950s scurrying for cover.

After the war Dr. Strobos studied under Anna Freud in London and came to the USA with her husband, a Fulbright-scholar. One of the reasons she stayed in the Unites States rather than returning to her native Holland was her distaste for the way in which wartime collaborators managed to maintain or gain key positions in business and government there after the war.

She started her own child and family psychiatry practice which she actively ran until 2009. Continuing in the tradition of ensuring safe shelter for those at risk, she founded a child psychiatry clinic in South Carolina for indigent patients and an assisted living facility for the recovering mentally ill in New York.

As a young mother living in the United States, Dr. Strobos suppressed her wartime experiences, and it was not until many decades later that she started sharing her history with others, including her children, who had heard about their mother's heroic deeds from their grandmother.

Recognition also came late. In 1989 Dr. Strobos was honored with the *Yad Vashem Righteous among the Nations* medal. She was repeatedly honored in the United States. It is unfortunate that her native country has shown so little interest in her wartime work there and that it was never officially acknowledged – but then the Dutch have shown repeatedly that once someone leaves the country permanently, they effectively cease to be of importance, an attitude that, we are sure, would be abhorrent to Dr. Strobos, who had room in her house for everyone, regardless of nationality, ethnic background, or religious affiliation.

On February 27, 2012 at the age of 91, Dr. Tina Strobos died in Rye, New York, of cancer.

May/June 2012

Resistance Hero
Guided by Unshakeable Faith
Diet Eman (1920-2019)

Diet Eman was a deeply religious woman. It was her strong faith that guided her in life. Despite the many hardships and sorrows she suffered, it seems that she never doubted that God had a purpose for her, that everything was ordained by His will and had a divine reason, however opaque or unfathomable that higher purpose might seem to a human being.

When the Germans invaded the Netherlands in 1940, she was engaged to Hein Sietsma, her soulmate, and a fellow Christian of unshakeable faith. As is common in the Reformed tradition to which both Diet and Hein belonged, they dove deep into scripture to determine what their course of action should be, how they could best serve the Lord under the new tyrannical National-Socialist regime, which had replaced their beloved Queen Wilhelmina.

According to Matthew 22, Jesus said 'Render therefore unto Caesar the things which are Caesar's; and unto God the things that are God's.' And the apostle Paul clearly writes in Romans 12: 'Let every soul be subject unto the higher powers. For there is no power but of God: the powers that be are ordained of God. Whosoever therefore resisteth the power, resisteth the ordinance of God: and they that resist shall receive to themselves damnation.' These Bible verses formed a real dilemma for many Dutch Reformed Christians. Did these verses tell them to accept the German authorities and forbid them to resist the occupation? But Diet and Hein in their studies concluded, as did many of their co-religionists, that Queen Wilhelmina was the rightful divinely ordained higher power. And as such, they felt it was not a sin, but indeed their Christian duty, to resist the Nazi regime.

They started relatively small, although what they did was not without danger. They copied news items from the forbidden English radio broadcasts and distributed them. But as the regime became more brutal and the persecution of the Jews began, Hein and Diet got deeply involved in the resistance against the Nazis. They found hiding places for Jews and distributed falsified IDs and ration cards. Together they saved the lives of several dozen persecuted Jews. The punishment for these types of activities was either the death penalty or incarceration in a concentration camp, which was essentially a slow, more cruelly drawn-out version of the former.

On April 26th, 1944, Hein Sietsma was arrested. He perished in Dachau concentration camp in December of the same year. Diet did not find out about his death until after the war. She and Hein were engaged early on in the war but had postponed marriage because they had wanted to proclaim their love publicly, before the eyes of their respective families and their congregation. That was impossible because of their clandestine activities. After the war, Diet said that had she known what was to happen to Hein, they would certainly have married in a smaller, more private ceremony.

Diet was also arrested and she spent time in Scheveningen prison and Vught concentration camp. She pretended to be a little dimwitted and had so many close calls during her arrest and interrogations, that she was sure that divine intervention was in play. Eventually, she was released and survived the war.

After the war she could not stay in Holland because of the trauma and ghosts of the past. *Royal Dutch Shell*, Hein Sietsma's former employer, posted her to Venezuela where she worked as a nurse. There, she met a Jewish American whom she married and followed to New York. When the couple had a dispute over the faith in which their children should be raised, she divorced him and moved to Grand Rapids in Michigan. She never spoke about the war, too deep was her trauma, until in 1978 she heard fellow resistance hero and camp survivor Corrie ten Boom speak, and started thinking about her duty to share her experiences. Her psychologist and her son also thought it could be therapeutic.

In 1990, she appeared at a symposium at *Dordt College* in Sioux Center, where Professor James Schaap convinced her to let him help her write a book about her wartime experiences. Together they published *Things We Couldn't Say* in 1994. It is a powerful memoir, combining letters, diary fragments and narrative. In 1998, *Yad Vashem* awarded her the *Righteous among the Nations* award.

When King Willem-Alexander visited Grand Rapids in 2015, he called her "one of our national heroes". He took her hand and spoke at length with her. Despite her traumatic life, she showed that she retained a strong sense of humor. When asked what the king had spoken about for such a long time, she answered, using an old Dutch idiom: "How would I know, I'm as deaf as a quail."

On September 3rd, 2019, resistance hero Diet Eman died. She was ninety-nine years old.

January/February 2020

The Last Dutch Sobibor Survivor
Selma Wijnberg (1922-2018)

Nineteen trains were sent to Sobibor death camp from the Netherlands, carrying 34,313 Dutch Jews. Only eighteen of them survived the war, most of them because they only spent a few hours in Sobibor before being selected for work in other concentration camps. Only two, Ursula Stern and Selma Wijnberg, actually spent time incarcerated in the camp.

Selma was born in Groningen and moved to Zwolle with her family when she was seven years old. She was known as Sarah or Saartje at the time, and she lived an uncomplicated happy life in the kosher hotel that her family ran near the Zwolle cattle market. Although the family were orthodox Jews in their religious practice, Selma remembered being thoroughly assimilated and having few, if any, Jewish friends.

Everything changed after the invasion of Holland by the Germans. In 1942, she decided to go into hiding, first in Utrecht, and then in nearby De Bilt. She was arrested on December 18th of the same year and was sent to concentration camp Vught in February 1943. In April, she was moved to transit camp Westerbork from where the trains to the east departed. She was there for a week before she was transported to Sobibor.

She remembered the overcrowded cattle cars as oppressively hot, especially because the prisoners were not given any water for the three days of the journey. When they arrived in Sobibor, she did not realize that by being selected for work in the camp, she escaped the fate of the overwhelming majority of her fellow passengers, who were sent to the gas chambers immediately upon arrival. That evening, she would be told by some fellow Dutch inmates what the huge fire that lit up the night sky, and the smell of burning hair and flesh signified.

For their own entertainment, the German camp guards had organized a party where the Jewish inmates were forced to dance with each other. A young Polish Jew called Chaim Engel asked Selma to dance. They fell in love and Chaim, experienced after six months in the camp already, protected her. Death was a daily danger. The slightest infringement, or even just getting sick, could mean a quick bullet to the head, being cruelly beaten to death, or being sent to the gas chamber. When Selma got typhus, she had to hide this to not be killed.

On October 14th, 1943, an uprising took place. Chaim was one of the organizers, but he did not tell Selma about the plans until the day of the revolt. Approximately three hundred prisoners attempted to escape, and although the uprising was carefully and meticulously organized, it failed because of unforeseen circumstances. Many prisoners were shot by SS guards or perished in the minefields around the camp. It is estimated that less than fifty escapees survived the war. Chaim and Selma were among them. They spent nine months hiding in the attic of a Polish farmhouse.

They had gotten married and had a baby boy, Emiel, when they set off for the Netherlands by way of Odessa and Marseille after the war. Emiel died during the journey of suspected food poisoning. He was buried at sea near Greece. The couple's reception in the Netherlands was hostile. Chaim was told that as a Pole he was an unwanted alien and not welcome to stay. A second official wedding did not help, but made matters worse. By marrying the 'alien Engel', Selma had become a Polish national in the eyes of the Dutch authorities and lost her own right to stay in the country of her birth. Chaim and Selma remained in Holland semi-clandestinely until 1951 when they immigrated to Israel. In 1957, after the Sinai War of 1956, wishing to escape war forever, the couple, now with two children who had been born in Holland, moved to the United States, where they eventually settled in Branford, Connecticut.

In the US, Selma and Chaim spoke in schools and community centers about their wartime experiences, to ensure the atrocities were not forgotten. They only returned to Europe to testify in war crime cases against the henchmen of Sobibor. It was not until 2010, seven years after Chaim's death in 2003, that Selma finally went back to Holland accompanied by two granddaughters. During her visit, the Dutch government officially apologized for the treatment she got after the war and presented her with a knighthood. She did not accept the apology – too little, too late.

She died on December 4th, 2018 in New Haven, Connecticut at the age of ninety-six. She was the last Dutch Sobibor survivor.

February/March 2019

Skating for Her life
Ellen Burka (1921-2016)

Ellen Burka vividly described falling in love with figure skating. It was well before the start of World War II when she was in her very early teens. She saw people performing pirouettes and jumps on the ice rink behind Central Station in Amsterdam. She was fascinated and wanted to be able to do that herself. Much to the initial chagrin of her staid, Victorian upper-middle class parents, Ellen would head out to the ice rink in working class East Amsterdam to practice with her best friend. By watching two Austrian coaches they improved their technique. The two girls became acquainted with two young men who were also enthusiasts, and the four performed stunning pairs routines, entirely self-taught, skating regularly at exhibitions throughout the country.

By the early years of the occupation, Ellen and her friends were skating on the new ice sheet in the Apollohal, an arena in Ellen's upscale South Amsterdam neighborhood. But one day as she walked over to the Apollohal for her regular skating practice, a new sign adorned the entrance: 'Forbidden for Jews'. Her heart sank. Her passion for skating had never abated, and skating gave her life meaning. But as we know now, much worse was to come. Ellen's mother had wanted to flee or go into hiding, but her father felt that as a successful businessman he would be spared. Yet disappear eventually they did, of course, never to return. Except for Ellen, thanks to her passion for figure skating and a split-second decision when she arrived at Westerbork Transit Camp.

A week after her grandmother had been hauled off to Westerbork, it was Ellen and her parents' turn. When she arrived, she had to go through the registration process. When asked for her occupation, she considered 'student' too boring and run-of-the-mill. So she said "Dutch national figure skating champion". This was stretching the truth. There were no national figure skating championships in pre-war Holland. But as Ellen would later say: "If there had been a championship, I would have won anyway, I was the best."

When camp commander SS-Obersturmführer Albert Gemmeker heard that he had a figure skating champion among his prisoners, he was ecstatic. He loved the sport and had Ellen send for her skates and outfit. She was put in a relatively easy work detail and served at soirees held in Gemmeker's villa. But even better, when winter came she was allowed to practice on a frozen pond near the camp. It was the first time she had skated since the Apollohal had been declared off-limits to Jews. What she was not allowed to do in Amsterdam, she could do at the concentration camp. Within two weeks of being sent to Westerbork, her grandmother and parents were deported to Sobibor, where they were gassed upon arrival. Eventually, Ellen was sent to 'model camp' Theresienstadt where many prominent Jews and other prisoners were sent. Circumstances were still atrocious there, and mortality high, but at least it was not a death camp.

There Ellen met her future husband Jan Burka, a Czech Jew. After the Russians liberated the camp, Ellen and Jan walked to Amsterdam to get married. The Canadian liberators could not wait to start playing hockey, and they immediately reinstated the ice sheet in the Apollohal. Ellen started skating there again and won two Dutch national championships, for real this time. Fearful of the communist menace, Jan persuaded Ellen to immigrate to Canada with their two young daughters, Petra and Astra. Against her will, Ellen acquiesced. After the couple divorced in the mid-1950s, Ellen, now a single mom, started coaching figure skaters in Toronto to make a living.

Ellen's passion for skating and her deep love of music and dance made her an outstanding coach. She demanded a lot from her students and is described by them as a strict disciplinarian. But she also emphasized freedom of expression and creativity on the ice. She is considered to have reinvented Canadian figure skating and to have infused it with a degree of style and artistic value unknown prior to her arrival. Using her unique combination of high demand for perfection and dedication, and her love of beauty on the ice, she coached numerous Canadian skaters, including her own daughter Petra, to Olympic medals and world championships. She continued to coach young skaters until she was ninety-three years old. She was awarded the *Order of Canada* and was inducted into the *Jewish Sports Hall of Fame.* Her achievements were never truly recognized in her native Netherlands.

Ellen Burka, figure skating legend and Holocaust survivor died on September 12th, 2016. She was ninety-five years old.

January/February 2017

Liberator and Father Finder
Lloyd Rains (1925-2013)

When Lloyd Rains and Olga Trestorff first met at a dance in Bloemendaal near her hometown of Haarlem, it was love at first sight. The dance took place in June of 1945 and was organized especially for Canadian troops stationed in the area. Dutch girls were very fond of Canadian soldiers in those days and, as would become all too apparent, the attraction was mutual.

Lloyd grew up on St. Joseph Island, Ontario and enlisted in the Canadian Army at the age of seventeen, serving in the *Princess Patricia Light Infantry*. He landed in Sicily with his unit and fought his way through Europe until he reached the Netherlands in April of 1945. When he met Olga at that dance, she was recovering from diphtheria caught during that disastrous last year of German occupation when thousands died of deprivation and starvation. Olga, like so many others, quite literally attributes her survival to the arrival of the Canadian liberators.

As Holland emerged from the ruins, Canadian military units remained in the country. With the large number of soldiers having to repatriate, troopship capacity was limited. The young, allied soldiers stationed in the Netherlands, mainly Canadians, were lonely, far away from home, and bored. They were also fit, exotic in a way, and seemed to have an endless supply of otherwise scarce articles such as cigarettes, chocolate, soap, and nylons. Despite the sorrow and trauma of five years of occupation – or probably because of it – the summer of '45 was party time for many. From lifelong romances to brief flings, Dutch girls and Canadian soldiers found each other. Almost 1,900 Dutch girls married Canadian soldiers and followed their husbands to Canada. Olga Rains-Trestorff was among them. She married

Lloyd on Christmas Eve 1945. Two weeks later he left for Canada, where Olga joined him in August of 1946.

But not all liaisons ended in marriage. Current estimates indicate that in those heady post-war months some seven thousand to eight thousand children were fathered by Canadian soldiers who soon left for Canada, often to go back to their Canadian wives or girlfriends.

This would probably have been of no immediate concern to Olga and Lloyd Rains, whose romance had blossomed and who lived happily in Peterborough, Ontario with their three sons, had they not visited the Netherlands in 1980. Lloyd and Olga traveled to Holland to take part in the 35th anniversary celebrations of the liberation at the invitation of the City of Amsterdam, his regiment having been the first to enter the city in May of 1945. As he and the other veterans paraded down the Dutch streets, he noticed something odd. Among the many cheering and waving spectators were quite a few people holding up placards with the text: 'Where are you, daddy?' Thirty-four or thirty-five years old by now, many of the 'liberation children' wanted to know who their father was, wanted to meet him, and were in search of answers to hitherto unanswered questions. In the strict, conservative atmosphere of the post-war era, many (but by no means all) of these children had been treated as outcasts. Some had been taken away from their mothers and raised in orphanages or foster homes. Some who had stayed with their mothers had been shunned by their extended families. Being a child born out of wedlock was a deep shame in Holland in the 1940s and 1950s. But by 1980, in a much different, much more liberal society, questions could be asked, blanks could start to be filled in.

Lloyd and Olga discussed the matter and decided that here lay a humanitarian task for them. They embarked on a quest, which they called *Project Roots* that would have them travel the breadth of Canada and the USA in a makeshift camper van, in search of lost fathers. The reception they got from the North Americans varied widely. Sometimes they were welcomed as the bearers of happy tidings about a long-lost romance and love child, sometimes they got doors slammed in their faces, sometimes they made phone calls where the only response was a long silence followed by a 'click'. More often the result of their efforts lay somewhere between these extremes: they were the catalysts in a journey of sometimes painful discovery by both parties in the reunion.

While Olga was the more visible member of the partnership, Lloyd did a lot of the research needed to find many of the missing men and supported Olga in any way he could. After a thirty-year quest Lloyd and Olga had traced four thousand liberation fathers, published three books, and had several documentaries and a TV drama miniseries made about their work. Lloyd and Olga, who had moved back to the Netherlands at the height of their Project Roots activities, in retirement settled in London, Ontario to be near their children.

Lloyd Rains, Canadian army veteran and father finder, passed away peacefully on Good Friday, March 29, 2013, after a 'liberation marriage' of sixty-seven years.

July/August 2013

Preacher and Teacher
Who Walked the Talk
Simon Kistemaker (1930-2017)

Although the Netherlands is now a thoroughly secular society, with among the lowest percentage of faithful in the world, the country was staunchly religious until quite recently. Dutch society was organized along denominational lines, with separate political parties, schools, universities, trade unions and even sports clubs for Catholics, and Protestants of different stripe. This societal principle was called 'pillarization'. In 1947, forty-two percent of the population was Protestant and thirty-eight percent Catholic, with the remainder representing Jews, other religions and the irreligious. The Protestants can be divided into two major groups, both Calvinist, one more liberal and the other more Orthodox. Unhelpfully, the Dutch names for the two groups 'Hervormd' and 'Gereformeerd' both translate to 'Reformed'. The Orthodox 'Gereformeerd' group represented about eight percent of the total population of the Netherlands in 1947. However, in the immediate large postwar emigration wave, they were significantly overrepresented among emigrants traveling to Canada. About one-third of Dutch immigrants to Canada in the period between 1947 and 1964 were 'Gereformeerd'.

Where Catholics and liberal Protestants quickly found spiritual homes in Canadian churches, the Orthodox reformed brought their 'pillar' with them and founded their own churches, schools, and colleges in Canada. In terms of theology, they found that they could quite easily connect with the institutions such as *Calvin College* set up in the USA by the followers of Dominie van Raalte, who founded Holland, Michigan with a group of early seceders from the mainstream Dutch Reformed Church.

Like all of Dutch society, the 'emigration associations' that enticed Dutch people to emigrate from postwar Holland on behalf

of the Dutch government, were organized along denominational lines. Among the many thousands of Reformed families that
emigrated to Canada was the Kistemaker clan, a farming family,
among them seventeen-year-old Simon. They settled in Hamilton, Ontario in 1947, and Simon soon followed his calling to
become a preacher. A logical path for him was to attend *Calvin Theological Seminary*, not too far from Hamilton, in Grand
Rapids, Michigan, where he taught Greek and Latin to support
his studies. He returned to the Netherlands in 1958 to obtain
his Doctorate in Theology at the Free University in Amsterdam,
the Orthodox Calvinist university founded by Abraham Kuyper
(1837 -1920), a former Dutch Prime Minister and a towering figure in modern Calvinist orthodoxy.

Kistemaker was ordained in 1961 and took up his post as minister at the *Christian Reformed Church* in Vernon, British Columbia. He served there until 1963, when he followed the call
to become a teacher. He went to Sioux Center in Iowa, where
he became Professor of Bible and Languages at *Dordt College*.
In 1971, he joined the faculty of the recently founded *Reformed
Theological Seminary (RTS)* in Jackson, Mississippi. When he retired in 1996, he continued to teach at the RTS, now at the Or-
lando, Florida campus.

Kistemaker was a highly regarded expert in evangelical theology, renowned for his seven books of New Testament commen-
tary, four of which won the *Gold Medallion Evangelical Book
of the Year Award*. Kistemaker was much admired and even
loved by his students, who felt he gave them deep insights into
scripture. In addition, he was admired for the way he lived his
life as a humble, serving, passionate Christian, despite his acclaimed stature within the evangelical community. He and his
wife opened their house to students, and many stayed with them
during their studies at RTS.

The advice Kistemaker gave his seminarians was simple and
clear: "know the biblical languages, Hebrew and Greek, an abil-

ity to read the Holy Scriptures in the original text pays off vast dividends in your preaching and teaching the word of God" and "spend much time in prayer and ask the Lord for wisdom and understanding".

Kistemaker was a loving husband and father and in his spare time enjoyed tending to his plot in the RTS community garden. His students remember him as an 'unfailingly gracious man, truly interested in his students'. Kistemaker himself said of his students: "Whenever I stand in front of a class of seminary students and consider their future, I see pastors and teachers. Behind them I envisage individual church members who are eagerly waiting to hear a full and accurate explanation of God's word. They want to know how Scripture can be applied significantly to their daily lives and occupations."

Kistemaker was a prime example of someone who followed the Kuyperian principle of applying God's word as he understood it in all walks of life. He 'walked the talk' in the truest sense of the word and was revered for it.

Simon Kistemaker died on September 23rd, 2018, in St. Petersburg, Florida. He was eighty-seven years old.

March/April 2018

Spiritual Father of De Krant
Gerard Bonekamp (1934-2021)

Without Gerard Bonekamp, there would be no *DUTCH the magazine*. For those readers among us who do not read *De Krant*, that statement may come as a surprise. Gerard was never involved with *DUTCH*, so for them his name may well be unknown or at best ring a distant bell. But it was Gerard who helped *Mokeham Publishing*, the publisher of both periodicals, off the ground.

Before the connection becomes apparent, we have to go back to 1969, to Vancouver, British Columbia. There, a Dutch travel agent and entrepreneur called Ryan Schlyecher launched a monthly publication called *De Hollandse Krant*. Its stated purpose was to provide the large group of relatively recent Dutch immigrants in British Columbia with news from their erstwhile home. An obvious secondary purpose was to promote his services in arranging travel to the motherland.

Schlyecher struggled under the weight of his responsibilities, and his health suffered. Twice, the paper skipped several issues as Schlyecher was being treated for heart problems. In 1976, when total collapse of the paper was imminent, Gerard Bonekamp stepped in. He purchased the paper from Schlyecher for a nominal sum – at the time it was, in the words of his son Gordon, "really nothing more than a list of subscribers."

Gerard was the proverbial right person at the right time. He was a schoolteacher by training and had immigrated to Canada in 1958 at the age of twenty-four with his wife Janny. He taught in the Christian school system that was deeply embedded in the Christian Reformed tradition as it had been brought to Canada by the immigrants of the 1940s and 1950s. After stints in London and Brampton in Ontario, and Edmonton in Alberta, Gerard became principal of the Christian School in Langley, British Columbia. A disagreement over the philosophical foundations of Christian education forced him out of his job and ultimately also out of his church. This happened just around the time that De Hollandse Krant was floundering.

Gerard realized that after between twenty and thirty years in Canada, most Dutch immigrants were not really concerned that much with Dutch current affairs but did still have a strong cultural affinity with their heritage. So he redesigned the paper in both form and content, as more of a monthly magazine, albeit still on affordable newsprint. He kept bringing some light news from Holland, but also included columns by fellow immigrants, letters to the editor, travel features and his own highly popular *Onder Ons* (Among Us) editorial.

He was an astute businessman and significantly extended his advertising base. His biggest coup possibly was getting De Krant (The Newspaper), as it was known by his readers, adopted by *Canadian Pacific Air Lines (CP Air)* as an 'in-flight service magazine' on its regular Vancouver to Amsterdam flights. With a twinkle in his eye, he would recount that he'd sit on a CP Air flight and watch with quiet contentment as all the passengers were reading 'his' newspaper. He was a determined, but modest man, and this was really the only recognition he sought.

Under his watch, De Krant developed from 'The Dutch Newspaper for the Pacific Northwest' to 'Monthly Magazine for Canadians and Americans of Dutch Origin', a tagline which the publication still uses. With a circulation exceeding 10,000 and a readership that was a multiple of that number (it was not unknown for several families to share one subscription, much to Gerard's acquiescent chagrin). Gerard could literally boast of having subscribers in all Canadian provinces and all American states.

On the editorial side, he made the insightful decision to bring his wife Janny on board. Together they made De Krant 'gezellig', and – an often-expressed sentiment by its readers – into one big family. For many readers, Gerard and Janny provided the only remaining connection with their land of birth, left behind decades before, and were loved for it (and I use that word advisedly).

In 2008, after a reign of thirty-two years, his printer gave him an ultimatum to deliver digitally or not be printed at all – he still pasted up the paper manually. Well into his seventies, he was not prepared to completely relearn the skills that he had honed over thirty-two years. Despite being intimately associated with 'his' paper, he allowed me to purchase his 'Krant'. I launched DUTCH, the magazine three years later, but De Krant is still going strong, in no short measure because of the foundation Gerard laid.

On January 16th, 2021 Gerard Bonekamp, the spiritual father of De Krant, died in Surrey, British Columbia. He was eighty-six years old.

May/June 2021

Philanthropist and Agribusiness Pioneer
Cor van Raay (1936-2021)

Cor van Raay had some valuable advice for young people choosing a career path. In a 2015 interview he said: "You never want to choose a career that you don't like doing. If you like what you're doing, you'll most likely be good at it, and you should do it. What's the worst-case scenario? If you go broke, so be it. If you choose something that someone forced you to do, or are doing something strictly for the money, you'll never be good at it." Cor van Raay was very good at what he did, and it follows from his own words that he enjoyed his work tremendously. He never went broke, although occasionally he came close!

Van Raay was born in Nijmegen in 1936. He came to Canada in 1959 because he wanted to be a farmer and felt that the opportunities in the Netherlands for the way he wanted to farm were insufficient. Starting out in landscaping in Vancouver, he realized his ambition of becoming a farmer soon after arriving: when he got the opportunity to take over a beet farm in Alberta he jumped at it. A driven businessman as well as a dedicated farmer, Cor soon expanded his land holdings and added other crops, such as barley, wheat and potatoes.

Cor really came into his own when he started buying cattle. He pioneered the large feedlots for which Alberta is renowned. By 2009, his operation covered 16,000 acres and employed one hundred people who managed more than 100,000 head of cattle – the largest feedlot in Canada. Cor let his entrepreneurial spirit guide him into ventures outside the huge family farm. He became co-owner of *Butte Graine Merchants* (a trucking and cattle feeding operation) and was also co-owner of a *John Deere* dealership for some time.

The long hours and visionary leadership that Cor put into his business – supported by his wife Christine and six children – lay at the root of his success. But as in everything in life, it wasn't all smooth sailing. When the first farm Cor and Christine owned in 1964 (all of 320 acres) struggled, Cor supplemented the family income by working in the oil fields and sawmills of northern British Columbia and Alberta. The cyclical nature of the market brought challenges, as did the protectionist tariffs that the United States levied on Canadian beef from time to time and the outbreak of diseases like Foot and Mouth. The biggest setback came in 2003 when a single case of BSE (Mad Cow Disease) in Canada prompted the US to close the border to all Canadian beef. But solid business planning, diversification and an unfailing entrepreneurial spirit ensured that the Van Raay operation survived the setbacks. By the time Cor decided to retire in 2009 and four of his kids took over the business, it had completely rebounded.

Cor was a leader in the Alberta agricultural community and was recognized with induction into the *Alberta Agriculture Hall of Fame* in 2016 and by being awarded an honorary doctorate by the *University of Lethbridge* in 2015.

Cor believed in giving back to the community, which he felt was instrumental in creating the circumstances for him to be successful, and he supported many southern Alberta charitable organizations. He made several multi-million dollar donations to the *Lethbridge YMCA*, which was subsequently named *West Lethbridge Cor van Raay YMCA* in his honor. A substantial donation in 2015 allowed the University of Lethbridge and *Lethbridge College* to found the *Cor Van Raay Southern Alberta Agribusiness Program*. When asked what results he would like to see ten years after his donation, he said: "Hopefully this money can be used to help us have well-educated farmers and more people getting excited about agriculture."

Of course Cor did not really retire. People that driven just don't. After the children took over the Alberta farm, with his new life partner (Christine had succumbed to breast cancer in 2005), Cor started afresh in Outlook, Saskatchewan, where he purchased a 35,000-acre farm growing lentils, wheat, barley and canola. Needless to say almost, of course this operation was highly successful, and John quickly became a valued member of the Outlook community, where he donated funds to many local causes.

Cor van Raay, agribusiness pioneer and philanthropist died on July 29th 2021. He was eighty-five years old.

January/February 2022

Distinguished American Scientist Celebrated Dutch Poet
Leo Vroman (1915-2014)

Leo Vroman was born in 1915 into a middle-class Jewish family in Gouda. His mother was a mathematics teacher, his father taught science. After graduating from the high school where his parents taught (now named after him) Leo went to the *University of Utrecht* to study biology. In the fall of 1938, in his third year, Leo attended an introductory event for freshmen at his student society, where he first saw Tineke Sanders, a medical student newly arrived from the Dutch East Indies. 'Oh my God, my wife,' he thought. Tineke's memories of their meeting are more prosaic: a kind man, but quite old. The two quickly became friends. One evening in November, Leo delivered the message: they could not just be friends, it had to be more. If she did not feel the same way, they could never see each other again. She asked for time, tried to imagine him sitting unshaven across from her at the breakfast table in his pajamas and thought: 'Yes that would work.' Three weeks after Leo's declaration, she wrote him a letter telling him she'd give it a try. Less than two blissful years later, they would be harshly separated for a long time.

On May 14th, 1940, four days after the German invasion of the Netherlands, Leo escaped the country. Tineke was too young to join him, her mother said. Leo made it to the Dutch East Indies, where he completed his biology degree. When the Japanese invaded, he was drafted into the army. After the Dutch capitulation, he spent three years in Japanese POW camps in Indonesia and Japan.

When the war was over, he decided to return to the Netherlands by way of New York. However, he did not make it back to Europe as planned, because he landed a job as a research assistant at *St. Peter's General Hospital*. He sent Tineke a telegram saying: 'I have great news: I am not coming back.' Tineke later said she was less than impressed by this 'great news'. She embarked on the *Queen Mary* and sailed to New York, where the two, who had not seen each other since May 14th, 1940, got married on September 10th, 1947, the day after she landed. Tineke joined the staff at St. Peter's and Leo and Tineke now also became colleagues.

Leo went on to become a successful research scientist, specializing in blood. He discovered a process that takes place in the blood just before it clots, which is named for him: the Vroman Effect. He published dozens of articles in medical and scientific journals and received several prizes and awards. But scientific articles about blood are not all that he published. He sketched, painted, and wrote poetry. Although he took US citizenship in 1951, Leo became a literary icon in his native country. He published more than fifty collections of poetry, a dozen or so works of prose, won every prestigious literary award that the Dutch have to offer, and received an honorary doctorate as well as a knighthood – all the while continuing to work as a scientist in the United States and, more importantly, living life with Tineke and their two daughters.

Not easily categorized, Leo Vroman was a genre himself – his works sometimes accompanied by his highly accomplished drawings. His use of the Dutch language was playful and vibrant, and he coined many new words. He speculated that his linguistic isolation – he only spoke Dutch with Tineke – laid the foundation for this phenomenon. A more likely explanation might be the possession and active use of an exceedingly creative mind.

Leo was a kind, helpful and generous man. When the editor of *DUTCH the magazine* approached him with the request that she be allowed to publish a translation of one of his poems, *Indian Summer*, he not only gave permission to use his work, he went a step further and created a new translation, *Indian Summer Again*, especially for the magazine. That was in the final stage of his life – a period he lived with as much curiosity about the world as he had when as a six-year-old he made his first "scientific discovery", as he put it himself, while sitting in the bathtub watching condensation on the bathroom wall form the pattern of brickwork under the paint. He had long been curious about death and the experience of dying. On February 22nd, 2014, his curiosity was satisfied. He died in Fort Worth, Texas where he and Tineke had lived since 1997 to be closer to their oldest daughter.

Distinguished scientist in America, celebrated poet and artist in the Netherlands, and the most devoted husband any wife could wish for, Leo Vroman lived for ninety-eight years. He was prolifically productive until the very end.

May/June 2014

Designer of the World's Most Beautiful Money
Ootje Oxenaar (1929-2017)

When the euro was introduced in the Netherlands on January 1st 2002, the Dutch lamented losing their stable and ancient currency, the guilder. They also lost the most modern and beautiful money in the world. The fifty-guilder bill with its bright yellow and orange Van Gogh inspired sunflower theme probably still stands out as the most remarkably noticeable banknote ever produced. It was part of a series of three nature and landscape inspired bills. The one-hundred-guilder bill showed a common snipe on one side and a water snipe on the other, and the stunning deeply purple 250 guilder bill had a lighthouse as its focal design feature and was generally considered by the Dutch public as the most beautiful of the series. Although the Dutch loved their paper money, many foreigners – unaccustomed to the occasional progressive tendencies of the Dutch establishment – considered the brightly colored unorthodox bills to be 'Monopoly money'. This is not altogether surprising when one considers that their designer himself once said that money worldwide was uninspiring and "muddy in color", and that the only money that really inspired him when he started designing banknotes was "play money, like Monopoly money".

Even before this series of banknotes was launched with the 'snipe' in 1977, the Dutch Central Bank had stood out with its design of a brightly colored series of notes, which showed – more traditionally – national cultural icons (playwright Vondel, painter Frans Hals, composer Sweelinck, naval hero De Ruyter and philosopher Spinoza). However, the portraits of the national heroes had an almost cartoon-like quality, nothing like the traditional portraiture of banknotes. These banknotes played an important role in establishing 'Dutch Design' as a tradition to be emulated worldwide.

The graphic artist and Monopoly money admirer responsible for these two series of bills was Robert Deodaat Emile ('Ootje') Oxenaar. Oxenaar was born in The Hague in 1929. He graduated from the *Royal Academy of Art* in his birthplace in 1953 and went on to become a lecturer there and eventually professor of visual communication at the *Technical University of Delft*. In addition to making banknotes, he was also a prolific designer of posters, book covers and postage stamps. The latter role culminated in his successful tenure at the Dutch postal service (PTT) as Director of Art and Design.

Oxenaar was not only an accomplished and creative designer, he also had a humoristic and slightly rebellious streak. His banknotes – which, by the way, were among the most secure of the era with an abundance of safety features – contained many hidden references. On the very first bill he was commissioned to design in 1966 (which was more conventional and predated the cartoonish 'cultural icons' series) he printed his name in the frieze of a temple – sacrilege, some said. On the Spinoza one-thousand-guilder bill, one of Oxenaar's fingerprints is hidden in the philosopher's wavy hair. The lighthouse on the purple 250-guilder bill has three names written on it in minuscule print: the names of three special women in Oxenaar's life, including his granddaughter. The watermark in the same bill is a rabbit. Why a rabbit? Oxenaar saw his girlfriend's rabbit hopping through the backyard as he was designing the bill. As secure a watermark as any and fitting with the nature-themed design, he thought, and the rabbit made it onto the bill.

In his designs he never forgot about the utilitarian aspects of his work. He chose fonts, for example, that were bold and instantly legible. Design was more than only art to Oxenaar. Designs had to combine form and function. His view of design influenced corporate design in the Netherlands for decades and to a certain extent still does.

When in 2000 his wife Dawn Barrett was appointed Dean of

Architecture and Design at the *Rhode Island School of Design (RISD)* in Providence, Oxenaar followed her and emigrated to the United States. There he also taught at the RISD, in the graphic design department.

Banknote designer Ootje Oxenaar died on June 13th 2017 in Manomet, Massachusetts where he lived with his wife. He was eighty-seven years old.

September/October 2017

Painter with Fabrics
Koos van den Akker (1939-2015)

All Koos van den Akker needed was a sewing machine. He created his first dress (for his sister) on a simple, old sewing machine from a bedsheet. When he was conscripted into the Dutch army – generally not a happy place for a young, gay man in the 1950s – his talents were immediately recognized. He spent his two years behind a sewing machine rather than a rifle, sewing dresses for officers' wives. It was with a sewing machine and $180 in his pocket that he arrived in New York City from the Netherlands in 1968. He sold his creations from his hotel room in the Village. And it was behind a sewing machine, as he said in 2013, that he wished to die. His wish was almost fulfilled. He sewed until three weeks before his death of colon cancer.

At the age of fifteen he already knew that all he wanted to do was to create beautiful clothes. He was admitted to the *Royal Academy of Art* in The Hague, three years before the customary minimum age of admittance, which was eighteen. After the academy and conscription, Van den Akker went to Paris to work for Christian Dior. He returned to his native The Hague, where he opened a boutique. He was not happy. A few years before his death he told an interviewer that the Dutch women he worked for lacked every sense of style. Almost fifty years later, he still had not shaken it off: "I hate Holland, I hate Dutch people too. I really have a hard time with them," he said. The move to New York gave him a great sense of relief and freedom.

Van den Akker's creations are instantly recognizable. His style is highly personal and is defined by the use of many different colors and patterns in a single article of clothing. His designs were a hit among the rich and famous. His long list of celebrity clients included Elizabeth Taylor, Cher, Brooke Shields, Barbara Walters, Gloria Vanderbilt, Isabella Rossellini, Stevie Wonder, Magic Johnson and Harry Belafonte. Inevitably, his store on Madison Avenue was a favorite destination for many New York socialites. Although Koos was already an established supplier of clothing to the elite, his biggest break came when Bill Cosby decided that Van den Akker's sweaters would become the signature clothing of his *Cosby Show* character, Dr. Huxtable. It all happened by accident. A mutual friend, singer Josephine Premice, once was stuck for a birthday present for Cosby. She asked Van den Akker to make a sweater. Cosby liked it so much that he wore it during the taping of an episode of the show. After that he ordered fifteen others and the 'Cosby sweater' became an icon, and Van den Akker's biggest success. No one who watched the Cosby show in the 1980s could have missed the stylish and unique sweaters that the main character wore.

Van den Akker's clothes sold for thousands of dollars apiece. Mass produced versions were on sale at upscale stores such as *Saks Fifth Avenue, Macy's*, and *Bloomingdale's*.

Despite his fame, and an honorary doctorate from the *San Francisco Academy of Art College*, he eschewed the trappings of fame and the designations that came with his success. He continued to work in his small studio in the Garment District and said: "I am not a fashion designer, I am a seamstress. I sew, that is what I do and that is what I have done my entire life. Fashion and the fashion world, I couldn't care less. It's so overrated and silly."

Mismanagement and a change in fashion favoring simpler monochrome colors in the early 1990s left Van den Akker with a big tax debt, collapsing sales and the threat of bankruptcy. He sold his company to a businessperson, something he had never been, and had never wanted to be. He became an employee in his own company and continued to create garments labeled with his name, *Koos*. Garments that were the result of his particular style, which he described as 'painting with fabrics'.

Two years before his death, Van den Akker said: "It's a rich life, it's a rich career. If I drop dead tomorrow, I've really done it all. I've made a lot of people happy."

Koos van den Akker, painter with fabrics and the creator of the Cosby sweater, died on February 4th 2015. He was seventy-five years old.

July/August 2015

Jewish. Woman. Leftist. Historian.
Evelien Gans (1951-2018)

Her parents left the Netherlands in 1951. The Korean War had just broken out, and Evelien Gans's father was convinced World War III was about to start. As a Jew who had survived the previous World War by going into hiding from the Nazis, he was not going to take any chances. His wife was pregnant with Evelien, who was born in New York City.

Although her dad was Jewish, according to the Halacha, Jewish Religious Law, Evelien was not. She had three Jewish grandparents, but her mother was not Jewish, so neither was she. About that she said: "I decide who I am. The most important part of my Jewish identity consists of my family history and Jewish history and culture in general. Micro and macro. And if I had been born six years earlier, I would have been gassed." To that she added: "Besides, I'm not only Jewish, but also a woman, a leftist and a historian."

Her childhood was defined by being on the move all the time "as if my father was just reliving his many hiding places during the war." Back in the Netherlands, Gans went to university to study history. She became involved in the radical student movement of the early 1970s, and an iconic photograph exists of her being arrested during riots in Amsterdam's Nieuwmarkt neighborhood, protesting against the demolition of a large part of the district for the construction of a new subway line. The photograph was proudly displayed in her hallway until her death.

She quit her studies because she "did not want to become a history teacher, but work with working class kids." She taught dramatic expression in vocational schools. These were exponents of early streaming in the class-based Dutch educational system at the time, where girls were taught home economics and boys basic technical skills. Toward the late 1970s, she became active in the radical squatters' movement and worked in a shelter for runaway girls.

But she came to dislike the fragmentary nature of her life and went back to university to complete her studies in 1985. She was fascinated by her family's stories of the war and the Holocaust. Just as she returned, a working group had been formed at the Dutch *Institute for War Documentation*, which was to research why more Jews from the Netherlands had been deported to extermination camps than from anywhere else in Western Europe, a question that had also been on Gans's mind. She immersed herself in Jewish history and published her first, controversial, book in 1994, *Goy Spite and Jewish Narcissism*, in which she explores the strained relationship between Jews and non-Jews in the Netherlands.

When her one-thousand-page Ph.D. thesis *The Small Differences That Decide a Life* about Zionists and Jewish Social-Democrats appeared, she had established a name as one of the foremost authorities in recent Jewish history. In 2002, she was awarded a chair at the *University of Amsterdam* in 'Contemporary Judaism, its history and culture'. She was a prolific writer, and in 2016, she published her seminal work *The Holocaust, Israel and "the Jew": Histories of Anti-Semitism in Postwar Dutch Society*.

"The public at large is interested in a history of extremes," she once said when she talked about having to avoid stereotyping when writing about Jewish history. "But of course there have been many more average Jews than Spinozas, Einsteins and Woody Allens." Elaborating on her analysis of the futility and inherent danger in stereotyping, she said: "Since Israel has developed into a military force, where Jews are not only doctors, merchants or artists, but also farmers and soldiers, a nation that fights wars, ends hostage-takings and has a secret service with a worldwide reputation, you do not hear much anymore about 'the cowardly Jew'."

Her relationship with Israel was ambivalent. Gans was proudly culturally Jewish and had strong relationships among, and admiration for left-wing circles inside Israel. She vehemently opposed the parallels Palestine leaders and their fellow travelers drew between Nazis and Zionism. "Equating Zionism with Nazism is a pure form of anti-Semitism. Terrible things happen in Israel, but there is no policy that drives toward a 'final solution'," she said, "it would be good to clearly differentiate between anti-Semitism, anti-Zionism, and anti-Israelism."

After several months of suffering from severe depression, Evelien Gans took her life on July 18th 2018. She was sixty-seven years old.

January/February 2019

The Best Goal Keeper
Never to Play in the World Cup
Jan van Beveren (1948 – 2011)

Dutch immigrants have come across the ocean for many reasons over the past few centuries but being bullied by Dutch Soccer legend Johan Cruyff must class as one of the more peculiar ones. Still, that is what people say brought Jan van Beveren first to Florida to play for the *Fort Lauderdale Strikers* and then on to Texas to play for the *Dallas Sidekicks*.

Jan van Beveren was the best Dutch goalkeeper ever to guard the 192 square foot plane of thin air that opposing players need to put the ball through to score a goal in soccer. There was not a spot in that area that Jan could not reach with his athletic jump. Jan's place was in the goal. His job was to make sure the ball did not penetrate that two-dimensional plane and the best way to do that was to rely on his unrivalled reactions. To defend it he did not often need to leave the goal like some other keepers do. That would have exposed him and his team to danger from lobs and combinations. He moved along the goal line and followed the ball with his eyes until it was his time to reach, jump, or dive and grab it.

Despite his unsurpassed qualities as a keeper Jan only played for the Dutch national team 32 times. He missed both 1970s World Cup series in which the Dutch team reached the final, in 1974 in Germany and in 1978 in Argentina.

Jan played for *PSV Eindhoven* from 1970 until 1980, but the national side was dominated by players from *Ajax Amsterdam*, including legends Cruyff, Neeskens and Krol. Cruyff was not only the lynchpin in the Dutch national squad – which dazzled soccer fans across the world with their particular style of soccer, dubbed 'total football' by coach Rinus Michels – but with his father-in-law, diamond salesman and sports broker Cor Coster, also dominated the business side of soccer in the Netherlands. This control on the field and in the boardroom resulted in an influence over the strategy and tactics of the squad that left little leeway for other players to follow their own instincts. When Jan van Beveren and his PSV-teammates decided that they did not want Coster to represent them, and when they questioned the different standards that successive coaches applied to Cruyff and his cronies in and around the field, the fight was on. An unequal fight that effectively barred the best goalkeeper Holland ever had from playing in two World Cup finals.

Several players in the squad, including former super star René van de Kerkhoff claim that with Van Beveren in goal Holland would have been world champions twice in the 1970s. We will never know that for sure of course, but in 1980 Van Beveren had had enough. A gentle, friendly man who knew that his participation in the Dutch game was at the mercy of a power beyond his control went into soccer exile. He never played for the Dutch national squad again.

After three years in Fort Lauderdale, he moved to Texas in 1983, where he stayed after his stint with the Dallas Sidekicks. He started a business in collectible postage stamps and lived, away from the limelight, with his wife Toosje and sons Raymond and Roger. He remained active on the field. He is remembered fondly by many local soccer players for his coaching and support. The last four and a half years of his life he was with *Spindletop Select Soccer Club* in Beaumont, Texas. There he did, in the words of a representative of the club "what he loved most: teaching soccer to youth in its most basic, purest form. Jan brought his love, knowledge and passion of the game to Beaumont, Texas, where he taught kids the most fundamental things about life ... and about soccer."

Jan was found slumped over his computer on June 26, 2011. He was only 63 years old.

September/October 2011

The Man Who Put
American Speed Skating on the Map
Peter Schotting (1943-2020)

L ong-track speed skating has never really taken off in North America, or anywhere else in the world for that matter. It is a sport that (at least at grassroots level) only thrives in the Netherlands. Even the Scandinavian countries of Norway and Sweden, where the sport did have popular appeal for most of the 20th century, seem to have given up on it. Except for the Dutch skating aficionados – and that means a sizeable proportion of the population of the Netherlands – there is little to enjoy in watching long-distance races like the five and ten-kilometers, where two lone skaters circle a four-hundred-meter track for minute upon dreary minute. An American sports journalist is reputed to have said, while he was covering the Olympics and was forced to narrate a speed skating event, that it was like watching grass grow. The Dutch know different, of course. And so do a tiny handful of Americans and Canadians. But they could not stop the Richmond four-hundred-meter oval from being stripped of its ice surface within weeks of the end of the 2010 Vancouver Olympics. There are only four covered four-hundred-meter ovals in all of North America, two in the USA and two in Canada. In tiny Holland, there are nine.

Nevertheless, the USA and Canada have produced their fair share of champions. Foremost among them, of course, is Eric Heiden, probably the best speed skater ever to have competed on the international circuit. His five gold medals in the 1980 Olympics, a clean sweep of the speed skating events, still stands as an extraordinary and singular achievement. Other great names spring to mind: Sylvia Burka was the first Canadian to win a Speed Skating World Championship, and Quebecker Gaetan Boucher took two gold medals at the Sarajevo Olympics in 1984.

There are other world champions, such as Eric Flaim and Sheila Young, and there is Olympic gold medal winner Peter Mueller. One thing these skaters all have in common is that they were once coached (and in many cases discovered) by Peter Schotting.

Schotting was an idiosyncratic and demanding speed skating coach. Always interested in sports and a later alumnus of Dutch sporting college *CIOS*, Schotting discovered speed skating while he was conscripted in the Dutch army in the late 1950s. He tried out the sport, but discovered that although he loved it, he was not very talented as a participant. He turned to coaching and became the head coach of the *Deventer Speed Skating Club* in 1966. Its home ice was at the renowned *IJssel Stadium*, the second oval with artificial ice in the Netherlands, and until its demolition in 1992, the venue of several prestigious international tournaments.

Schotting was a driven pioneer. In 1970 he managed to get his club invited to the famed and mysterious Medeo oval in Kazakhstan, which was generally off limits to westerners and where the Soviets trained and broke world record after world record at incredible speeds. After he ran afoul of Dutch skating authorities about his suggestion to establish a dedicated national sprint team, a discipline he led within the association, he went to Austria to develop its fledgling speed skating team. He did gain some notoriety as Austria's team coach, but not because of the achievements of his skaters. He was dragged off the ice by three Swedish policemen when he continuously flouted the directive to remain behind the red coaches' line on the ice during the World Championship in Gothenburg in 1971.

He moved to the USA in 1972 and settled near the only four-hundred-meter oval with artificial ice in North America at the time, in Milwaukee suburb West Allis. There he became the head coach of the Canadian national team, which had their permanent home in Milwaukee because it was the only place on the continent with guaranteed ice, although still outdoor in those days. Switching between coaching jobs in the USA and Canada, Schotting recruited short-track skaters into the long-distance branch of the sport, with an absolute apex when together with Dianne Holum he coached Heiden to his five gold medals and a total of seven senior world championships. After a brief stint with the Australian national team, he returned to the US, where he more or less disappeared into obscurity. But Pat Seltsam, one of Schotting's skaters said: "If you are or were a speed skater in America, Peter Schotting has influenced your career."

Peter Schotting, the man who put American speed skating on the map, at least for a while, died on March 19th 2020. He was seventy-six years old.

July/August 2020

Not Always the Bad Guy
Rutger Hauer (1944-2019)

Rutger Hauer first burst onto the Dutch acting scene in 1968 as Floris van Rosemondt, a gallant Medieval knight who embodied good and fought evil. *Floris* was a nine-episode children's television series. In a society with only two television channels and a dearth of homegrown productions, Floris was an instant hit. The third episode drew 3.5 million viewers in a country of 12.5 million people. One of the top attractions was Floris himself. Smart, athletic, brave and played by a strikingly handsome, young, blond Hauer. Every boy wanted to be Floris, and every girl wanted to be with him. Although Hauer's acting was still a little stilted, steeped in the tradition of the stage where he had started a few years earlier with a regional ensemble, Floris catapulted Hauer into Dutch audiences' awareness. It also established the cooperation between three soon hugely successful artists who would work on many projects together: Hauer, director Paul Verhoeven and screenwriter Gerard Soeteman.

Next came *Turks Fruit* (Turkish Delight). Again a Verhoeven, Hauer, Soeteman joint effort. The movie, which was released in 1973, still is the most successful Dutch film of all time, with more than 3.5 million moviegoers seeing it. In the tradition of the early seventies, when taboos had to be broken, the film – based on a novel by iconoclastic Dutch author and visual artist Jan Wolkers – centers on the emotional and intensely sexual relationship between Erik (Hauer) and Olga (Monique van de Ven), who eventually succumbs to a brain tumor. Hauer bares all, quite literally, as the film abounds in nudity, but also emotionally, as he becomes Erik in the movie. His reputation is set, and he becomes an icon of Dutch cinema, playing in multiple other Verhoeven films, culminating in his starring role in *Soldaat van Oranje*

(Soldier of Orange), in which he plays war hero Erik Hazelhoff Roelfzema. Soldier of Orange was internationally acclaimed and paved the way for Hauer, Verstappen and Soeteman to make a go of it in Hollywood.

Hauer's American debut was in *Nighthawks* (1981), in which he plays a terrorist chased by a New York cop played by Sylvester Stallone. It was the first of many 'bad guys' played by Hauer. His appearance, especially his blond good looks, make for a perfect Nazi, as many casting directors seem to have decided over the years. Hauer, who, in typical Dutch fashion, did not mince his words and knew what he wanted, opened up about about squabbles and intrigue on the set of Nighthawks where he told Stallone in no uncertain terms that he would not stand for being bullied around. Stallone, who is not known to be a pushover himself, accepted Hauer's criticism, and Hauer's reputation among colleagues as a straight shooter was established. But despite this outspoken attitude of a man who knows what he wants, Hauer was also gentle, kind and charitable. He associated himself with and actively supported the *Red Cross*, the *Dutch Aids Foundation*, the *Sea Shepherd Conservation Society* and his own *Rutger Hauer Starfish Association* (supporting children and pregnant women with HIV/AIDS).

After Nighthawks came *Blade Runner* (1982), the movie that cemented Hauer's reputation in the USA. After that, he was in high demand, and his list of credits is extensive. Among many other accolades, he won a *Golden Globe* for his role in the mini-series *Escape from Sobibor* (1987), in which he played the leader of the anti-Nazi resistance among the camp inmates. Hauer was not always happy with the fact that he was sometimes stereotyped as the archetypical 'bad guy', despite many heroic roles like the ones he played in Soldier of Orange and Sobibor. In interviews, he made abundantly clear that he regularly switched between 'good' and 'bad' guy roles.

That Hauer was an artist who knew what he wanted is not only apparent from the roles that he took, but also from those that he did not. He chose to turn down the role of the villain in the *James Bond* franchise at least three times because he did not like the one-dimensional aspect of the characters. He proposed a different type of adversary to 007, one that had the same sense of humor and was as sophisticated as Bond himself. That, he would have been interested in, he said, but the producers of the Bond franchise thought it was a crazy idea. So Bond would never meet Hauer.

Throughout his life Hauer "did what he enjoyed." Toward the end of his career that meant performing in low-budget and cult films. His reputation as a great actor afforded him that luxury. In 1999, the Dutch public voted him 'The best actor of the century'.

On July 19th, 2019 Rutger Hauer died in Beetsterzwaag in his beloved Friesland, where he started his acting career in 1967 with the *Noorder Compagnie* in Drachten. He was seventy-five years old.

November/December 2019

She Was Emmanuelle
Sylvia Kristel (1952-2012)

Sylvia Kristel's biography is depressing in its banal predictability. From the childhood neglect to the deadbeat older lovers, and from the success in a career-defining risqué role to an early death after a lifetime of living on the edge, we feel as if we know the plotline, even if the details are new to us.

The story starts in Utrecht, in 1952. Kristel grew up in a strict Catholic household, and just like in the rest of her life, the main protagonists can almost be filled in before one hears the actual tale of her youth: frigid mother, adulterous father, lecherous 'uncle' they're all there. Kristel was carted off to a convent school and the nuns took care of the rest of her education. It is no wonder then, that it made her say to her mother as she took part in a televised beauty pageant: "I've just got to be the prettiest and the most entertaining". She won the contest. She wanted to be noticed and she wanted to be a star. She wanted to be the center of attention after a childhood of emotional neglect and disinterest in her.

It was the early seventies and film makers were experimenting with how far they could go in representing eroticism in mainstream cinema without awakening the ire of the censors. A novice French filmmaker called Just Jaeckin was one of them. He was going to make a movie that would not make the viewer 'feel bad about feeling good', as the French posters for the film announced as it came out.

Jaeckin needed a leading lady, and when he spotted Kristel who had landed some modeling work after the pageant, he wanted to have her. As far as Kristel, 22 years old, was concerned he could, although she later said she chose the role for its artistic merits.

Jaeckin's movie, *Emmanuelle*, with Kristel in the title-role, became a huge success. Of course it was, like so many cultural phenomena, characterized more by the spirit of the time than by any revolutionary zeal by its makers to free the masses from their sexually repressing shackles. Kristel's assertion, later in life, that as Emmanuelle she "liberated European cinema" is of course an exaggeration. Besides, if she had not taken the role, Jaeckin would have found another aspiring starlet, prepared to do what it takes. But the movie must have been captivating in some sense: it ran for thirteen uninterrupted years on the Champs Elysees in Paris.

In the movie Kristel plays the wife of an older man whom she pleases with her subdued acquiescence in various sexual activities, involving a number of different partners both male and female. It sounds sordid, but shot with the soft focus and dimmed lighting that was in vogue in those days it could pass in a pinch for artistic, beautiful and enlightened. Kristel, who was not a very good actress and had never had any formal training in the craft, was at her best in Emmanuelle, possibly because here she really played herself. At least, after acting in sequel after sequel she seemed to reprise the role in real life. But the question in such circumstances always remains: did the role create the person, or did the person create the role? It is not as if Kristel had much of a choice. Emmanuelle, because of its runaway success – unconfirmed figures indicate that more than 650 million people saw the movie – had defined her. She had to accept that she would have to be Emmanuelle over and over again. At one point Kristel commented about some 'straight' roles she took: "I was dressed, but people preferred me naked". So she accepted roles in *Lady Chatterley's Lover*, *Mata Hari* and several other films that fit the genre.

Hugo Claus, the Flemish author and visual artist, who was famous throughout Holland and Flanders for his prolific literary output, was the first in a string of older men. But the relationship did not last, although it did give the couple a son, who was duly left to be raised by her mother, as Kristel set off for Hollywood. There she got into a downward spiral of alcohol and cocaine abuse. She got pregnant by English actor Ian McShane whose main claim to fame was his television role as duplicitous antiques dealer *Lovejoy*. After a drunken brawl with him she slipped down the stairs and lost the baby.

She married an aspiring French movie maker without any talent who got her to invest the big money she had made with the Emmanuelle movies in some of his no-hope schemes. She sold her houses in Los Angeles, Holland, Paris, and on the French Riviera to finance his hobby and ended up bankrupt.

Kristel was a heavy smoker, drinker and drug user and at 47 was diagnosed with throat cancer. She beat the disease with heavy courses of chemotherapy and radiation.

She was a successful painter and in her mid-fifties, back in Holland, she seemed to have her life on the rails. But then the cancer, which had been in remission for almost ten years, came back. It had spread to her liver. She embarked on another severe course of chemotherapy. On June 12, 2012 she was felled by a heavy stroke. Further chemotherapy was out of the question and four months later she died in her sleep.

On October 18, 2012 at the age of sixty, Sylvia Kristel died. She was Emmanuelle.

January/February 2013

The Most Famous Busker of The Hague
Chuck Deely (1954-2017)

The Hema Singer has died. For twenty years Chuck Deely was a welcome fixture on Grote Markstraat in The Hague. The Detroit-born busker arrived in the city in 1996 after extensive travels through Germany, Austria, Switzerland, Spain and his native USA. Charles Edward Deely III had an unfortunate childhood. His music-loving mother died in childbirth when Chuck was only seven years old. His baby sister died, too. His father remarried, but his stepmother got rid of the piano Chuck had played with his mother. It was too noisy, even though it was way down in the basement. Chuck resented that.

In 1973, drafted into the army, Chuck found himself in Germany, not Vietnam, to his own relief. He married a Yugoslav woman, whom he divorced after five years. A wandering life followed, playing the guitar in various bands, none of them really famous. But Chuck was a good singer and guitar player, with a high-pitched raspy voice in the style of Bob Dylan, whose *Like a Rolling Stone* was one of Chuck's signature tunes.

Playing in Tenerife in the late '80s, Chuck met a Dutch girl. When he got into trouble with the Spanish immigration authorities, he moved to Holland. and that is where he would stay. His girlfriend did not want to return to the Netherlands, and she never followed him.

Chuck started busking in the streets of The Hague, essentially, as he said himself, "to pay the rent".

For a few years there was no rent to pay. Chuck had fallen on hard times – hard, even in comparison to his earlier status as a musician living off the proceeds of busking – and spent two years living rough, on the streets, addicted to heroin and cocaine. But he managed to pull himself up by his bootstraps, found an apartment, kicked his heroin habit (he did admit to continued occasional cocaine and marijuana use), and kept busking. Chuck was proud that he had remained financially independent. He never claimed welfare and always paid his own way. He had a fixed routine, starting at The Hague's Central Station around 7:00 a.m. and playing the shopping precincts around Grote Marktstraat until he had earned enough money for the day, usually around 11:00 a.m., but occasionally not until the shops closed at six. His regular spot in front of archetypal Dutch department store *Hema* gave him his nickname.

Chuck did a brisk trade in his self-produced CDs, containing both covers and original songs. He was well-loved by the shoppers, and, uncharacteristically, the shopkeepers of The Hague. When in 2008 a policeman fined him for 'busking without a permit', a spontaneous collection took place by the businesses around the spot where he had been playing, to pay the fine. The mayor of The Hague at the time, Jozias van Aartsen, reacted by awarding Chuck a lifetime permit to busk in the streets of The Hague. This stood him in good stead when some years later the city was inundated with Eastern European scammers who pestered shoppers with their atonal musical offerings, aggressively demanding money. A blanket ban on busking was enacted. But Chuck, his lifetime permit in hand, could continue playing. As he said: "I hope they perceive me as a musician, and not as a beggar." He need not have worried about that. He had become an iconic part of downtown The Hague. Several documentaries were made about him, and he played with the *Residentie Orkest* (the The Hague Philharmonic) on two occasions. But despite a handful of television performances, he never made it off the streets, although he did occasionally get some extra financial support from well-wishers.

In late 2016, he was felled by the flu. Feeling compelled to head out into the winter cold to make a buck to pay for his upkeep, he fell seriously ill while performing outside. He was rushed to hospital, where he died. He was cremated, and his ashes were returned to Detroit to be buried in the family grave. He had not been back there since 1985. His death caused a great outpouring of grief in The Hague, complete with a very well-attended commemorative tribute concert – a show of solidarity that may have been a little late.

Chuck Deely, the most famous busker of The Hague, died on January 9th 2017. He was sixty-two years old.

May/June 2017

The King of Tapping
Eddie van Halen (1955-2020)

On January 26th 1955, Edward Lodewijk van Halen was born in Amsterdam. He moved to Nijmegen with his family as an infant, where he spent his early youth. His father Jan van Halen was a jazz pianist, clarinetist, and saxophonist. Inspired by their father's love for music, Edward (or Eddie) and his brother Alex began to play the piano at the age of six. In 1962, when Eddie was seven years old, the Van Halen family moved to California after receiving glowing letters about the US from relatives who had emigrated before them. They arrived in Pasadena with a few suitcases, fifteen dollars and a piano. While living in Pasadena, the brothers would commute forty miles to San Pedro, right through metro Los Angeles, to study piano with their elderly Lithuanian piano teacher Stasys Kalvaitis. Eddie's parents wanted the two brothers to become classical pianists but growing up in 1960s California it was almost inevitable that the boys would fall for rock music. Eddie's brother Alex bought himself a guitar, and Eddie followed in his footsteps and bought himself a drum kit. While Eddie was delivering newspapers to pay off his drum set, Alex would secretly play Eddie's drums.

When Eddie found out he blurted out: "Ok, you play drums, and I'll go play your guitar." Rock fans around the world can be grateful to Alex van Halen, because Eddie would become one of the most skillful and innovative guitarists in Rock history. Eddie and his brother formed their first band, *The Broken Combs*, with three others, to play at school events in Pasadena. Eddie would later say that the day of his very first performance, at a function at his own school, *Hamilton Elementary*, was the day he realized he wanted to be a professional musician. In 1974, Eddie formed the band that would carry his last name. Its line-up changed several times over the years, but the Van Halen brothers were constants, being joined in 2006 by Eddie's eldest son Wolfgang – yes, named after Mozart – playing bass guitar. Van Halen started touring as the opening act for other bands. Their show was so electric and Eddie's guitar skills so impressive, that they soon topped the bill. Contemporary hard rocker Leslie West said of seeing Van Halen play in 1978: "Neal Schon said to me: 'Leslie, you gotta check out this kid who's opening for us, he plays guitar like an organ, like a Bach organ fugue.' I was totally taken aback – It was Eddie van Halen, and he impressed me the way Clapton impressed me."

Van Halen's eponymous debut album was released in 1978. It reached number nineteen in the *Billboard* Pop Music Charts and would go on to sell ten million copies in the United States. By 1982, Van Halen had released four more albums. The lead single *Jump* from his 1984 album *1984* remains Van Halen's only single to reach number one in the US. Between 1986 and 1995, Van Halen released four albums, every one of which reached number one in the charts. The 1991 album *For Unlawful Carnal Knowledge* also won the band a *Grammy* and an *AMA*. Eddie van Halen was an innovator, both in regard to his instrument and in how to play it. He designed many of his own guitars and had them made to his specifications. He was also influential in developing a style of guitar playing called 'two-handed tapping', in which fingers from both hands tap strings on the neck of the guitar. Although he did not invent the style, he was one of the first to develop it into a compositional tool and to use it for longer sections of music. The style took off, and many other rock guitarists adopted it.

In looking back on his career, Van Halen reflected on his influences: "I've always said Eric Clapton was my main influence, but Jimmy Page was actually the way I am, in a reckless-abandon kind of way."

Eddie was a family man, touring with his brother for almost

five decades and then inviting his teenage son to play on tour with him in 2006. Eddie Van Halen would say in an interview with CNN about his son: "He had rhythm, and I went 'Yes, God, thank you!'". After his death, Wolfgang said: "He was the best father I could ever ask for. Every moment I've shared with him on and off stage was a gift". Eddie Van Halen remained a fluent Dutch speaker and he appeared on several Dutch radio shows.

After his death, many music legends paid tribute to Eddie. Their assessment was unwaveringly glowing: "a trailblazer" (Paul Stanley, *KISS*), "a brilliant guitarist" (Steve Hackett, *Genesis*), "a great guitarist" (Brian Wilson, *Beach Boys*), "best guitar player who's ever lived" (country singer Kenny Chesney), "a bold innovator" (Michael Balzary, *Red Hot Chili Peppers*), "a huge inspiration" (Jon Bon Jovi) and so on and so forth.

On October 6th, 2020, Eddie Van Halen, the king of tapping, died of throat cancer. He was sixty-five years old.

January/February 2021

SELECTED BIBLIOGRAPHY

Blackburn, Robert, Ruth Piwonka, Rudolph Visser & Geoff Benton – *The Kinderhook Reformed Church, 300 Years of Faith and Community.* Kinderhook Reformed Church, 2012.

Brinks, Herbert J. – *Write Back Soon. Letters from Immigrants in America.* CRC Publications, 1986.

De Haan, Peter & Kerst Huisman (Eds.) – *Famous Frisians in America.* Friese Pers Boekerij, 2009.

Galema, Annemieke – *Frisians to America, 1880-1914. With the Baggage of the Fatherland.* Regio-Projekt Uitgevers, 1996.

Ganzevoort, Herman & Mark Boekelman (eds.) – *Dutch Immigration to North America.* The Multicultural History Society of Ontario, 1983.

Haring Fabend, Firth – *New Netherland in a Nutshell, a Concise History of the Dutch Colony in North America.* New Netherland Institute, 2012.

Jacobs, Jaap – *The Colony of New Netherland, a Dutch Settlement in Seventeenth-Century America.* Cornell University Press, 2009.

Krijff, J. Th. J. – *100 Years Ago, Dutch Immigration to Manitoba in 1893.* Electa Press, 1994.

Lucas, Henry S. – *Dutch Immigrant Memoirs and Related Writings.* William B. Eerdmans Publishing Company, 1997. (Originally Published in 1955).

Michel, Sara – *With This Inheritance, Holland, Michigan, the Early Years.* River Road Publications, 1984.

Nelson, Ed – *A History of Lynden.* Lewis Publishing Company, 1995.

Rains, Olga – *We Became Canadians.* Overnight Copy Service, 1984.

Pearson, Jonathan – *Three Centuries, the History of the First Reformed Church of Schenectady, 1680-1980, Volume I.* The First Reformed Church of Schenectady 1980. (First published in 1880 as 'Two Hundredth Anniversary of the First Reformed Protestant Dutch Church of Schenectady, N.Y.')

Renaud, Anne – *A Bloom of Friendship, the Story of the Canadian Tulip Festival.* Whitecap Books, 2004.

Rose, Peter G. – *Delicious December, How the Dutch Brought Us Santa, Presents and Treats.* State University of New York Press 2014.

Scheltema, Gajus & Heleen Westerhuijs (eds.) – *Exploring Historic Dutch New York.* Museum of the City of New York, 2011.

Schryer, Frans J. – *The Netherlandic Presence in Ontario, Pillars, Class and Dutch Ethnicity.* Wilfrid Laurier University Press, 1998.

Sharp Pontius, Kathryn, Gerald F. De Jong & J. Dean Dykstra – *Three Centuries, the History of the First Reformed Church of Schenectady, 1680-1980, Volume II.* The First Reformed Church of Schenectady 1980.

Shorto, Russell – *The Island at the Center of the World.* Vintage Books, 2005.

Sloot, Rosemary – *Immigrant, from the Postwar Netherlands to Canada in 21 Paintings.* Mokeham Publishing, 2022.

Speerstra, Hylke – *Cruel Paradise. Life Stories of Dutch Emigrants.* Mokeham Publishing, 2018. (Originally Published in 2005).

Speerstra, Hylke – *The Comfort Bird.* Mokeham Publishing, 2017.

Swierenga, Robert P. – *Dutch Chicago, a History of the Hollanders in the Windy City.* William B. Eerdmans Publishing Company, 2002.

Van Arragon Hutten – *Uprooted, The Story of Dutch Immigrant Children in Canada, 1947-1959.* North Mountain Press, 2001.

Van den Hoonaard, Will C. – *Silent Ethnicity, the Dutch of New Brunswick.* New Ireland Press, 1991.

Van Hinte, Jacob – *Netherlanders in America. A study of Emigration and Settlement in the Nineteenth and Twentieth Centuries in the United States of America.* The Historical Committee of the Christian Reformed Church, 2003. (Originally Published in 1926).

Van Immerseel, J.M. – *For a Better Life, the Story of Dutch Emigration from Rotterdam to Quebec City, April 26-May 5, 1952 Aboard the Sibajak.* Booksinternational, 2019.

VanderMey, Albert – *And the Swamp Flourished, the Bittersweet Story of Holland Marsh.* Vanderheide Publishing, 1994.

VanderMey, Albert – *To All Our Children, the Story of the Postwar Dutch Immigration to Canada.* Paideia Press, 1983.

VanderMey, Albert – *When Canada Was Home, the Story of Dutch Princess Margriet.* Vanderheide Publishing 1992.

White, Colin & Laurie Boucke – *The Undutchables, an Observation of the Netherlands: Its Culture and Its Inhabitants.* White Boucke Productions, 2019.

Widmer, Ted – *Martin van Buren, President of the United States of America, 1837-1841.* Times Books, 2005.

INDEX

BY MOKEHAM PUBLISHING

PERIODICALS

DUTCH THE MAGAZINE
A bi-monthly magazine about the Netherlands and its People, at Home and Abroad. Full color glossy in English. First issue published in September 2011.

MAANDBLAD DE KRANT
A monthly magazine for Canadians and Americans of Dutch Origin. Newsprint. Mostly in the Dutch language. First issue published in October 1969.

BOOKS

THE DUTCH IN WARTIME BOOK SERIES
TOM BIJVOET AND ANNE VAN ARRAGON HUTTEN (EDITORS)
The Dutch in Wartime, Survivors Remember is a series of books containing the wartime memories of Dutch immigrants to Canada and the USA, who lived through the occupation of the Netherlands in World War II.

Book 1: Invasion (ISBN 978-0-9868308-0-8)
Book 2: Under Nazi Rule (ISBN 978-0-9868308-3-9)
Book 3: Witnessing the Holocaust (ISBN 978-0-9868308-4-6)
Book 4: Resisting Nazi Occupation (ISBN 978-0-9868308-5-3)
Book 5: Tell Your Children About Us (ISBN 978-0-9868308-6-0)
Book 6: War in the Indies (ISBN 978-0-9868308-7-7)
Book 7: Caught in the Crossfire (ISBN 978-0-9868308-8-4)
Book 8: The Hunger Winter (ISBN 978-0-9868308-9-1)
Book 9: Liberation (ISBN 978-0-99919981-0-4)

THE COMFORT BIRD BY *HYLKE SPEERSTRA*
The Comfort Bird follows the experiences of three generations of two families of farm laborers from a small town in the Northern Netherlands. One family moves across the ocean and passes through Ellis Island in 1911, the second family is too much rooted in the heavy soil of the old country to emigrate. In a strange twist of fate World War II brings the families together again, on opposing sides of the conflict. The story is based in fact and author Hylke Speerstra traveled extensively in the USA, Germany and the Netherlands to research original sources and interview descendants.
(ISBN 978-0-99919981-1-1)

CRUEL PARADISE BY *HYLKE SPEERSTRA*
Cruel Paradise, Life Stories of Dutch Emigrants deftly weaves together the firsthand stories of men and women who emigrated from the Netherlands to Canada, the USA, Australia, New Zealand, and South Africa throughout the twentieth century. Often poignant, sometimes amusing, always memorable, these stories provide a moving tribute to those who left their homeland behind with little more than uncertain hopes for their children.
(ISBN 978-0-99919981-2-8)

IMMIGRANT BY *ROSEMARY SLOOT*
Immigrant, From the Postwar Netherlands to Canada in 21 Paintings tells an intensely personal, yet universal story in exquisitely detailed paintings. Rosemary Sloot writes in her artist's statement: 'Just prior to her death my strong, pragmatic mother quietly told us that she had only one regret and that was immigrating to Canada'. A huge shock to Sloot, who herself was born in Canada. The unexpected confession culminated in the collection of the 21 works that form Immigrant.
(ISBN 978-1-7774396-6-8)

Books, magazine subscriptions and single issues are available from dutchthestore.com.